Speaking Effectively

Strategies for Academic Interaction

Janet L. Kayfetz

University of California, Santa Barbara

with

Michaele E.F. Smith

University of California, Santa Barbara

Heinle & Heinle Publishers
A Division of Wadsworth, Inc.
Boston, Massachusetts 02116 U.S.A.

Vice President and Publisher: Stanley J. Galek
Editorial Director: David C. Lee
Assistant Editor: Kenneth Mattson
Production Supervisor: Patricia Jalbert
Manufacturing Coordinator: Lisa McLaughlin
Project Management and Design: Chernow Editorial Services, Inc.
Cover Illustration and Design: Lisa Sheehan, Bortman Design Group

For permissions, see p. 145.

Library of Congress Cataloging-in-Publication Data

Kayfetz, Janet L.
   Speaking effectively : strategies for academic interaction / Janet
L. Kayfetz with Michaele E.F. Smith.
     p.   cm.
   ISBN 0-8384-2276-4
   1. English language—Textbooks for foreign speakers. 2. English
language—Spoken English. 3. College students—Language. 4. Oral
communication. I. Smith, Michaele E.F. II. Title.
PE1128.K385 1992
428.3'4—dc20   92-3958

Heinle & Heinle Publishers is a division of Wadsworth, Inc.

Manufactured in the United States of America.

ISBN 0-8384-2276-4

10 9 8 7 6 5 4 3

Contents

Chapter 2 Asking Questions and Reformulating Questions 17

Chapter 3 Making a Request and Granting a Request 27

Chapter 9   Giving an Unrehearsed Talk   139

Preface

This book concerns itself with two important and interrelated dimensions of speaking effectively. The first is that speaking is an activity that is always an integrated part of social behavior. Each time that people speak together, in addition to making choices about what they are going to say, they must also decide how formal, how deferential, how direct, and even how silent they should be. They make these choices so that their "speaking behavior" fits the norms of interaction for the social situation in which they are participating.

The second dimension of speaking effectively is that people who speak together create an interdependent flow of discourse that takes its shape with each speaking turn. People who speak together do not follow a "pre"-formulated script; instead, they respond to what others really say or imply. If the discourse unfolds in a way that is not anticipated or desired, each person must be able to adapt and respond appropriately. This ability to speak responsively and flexibly is as important a part of effective speaking as is the related skill of using language that is appropriate to the social situation.

The activities in this book bring into focus these two core dimensions of speaking effectively. With guidance, students will begin to recognize the interactive patterns as well as the social norms of speaking and will develop a competence and confidence for speaking that is genuine, flexible, and truly effective.

——— Recommendations to the Teacher ———

Each chapter emphasizes an important aspect of speaking used in social situations with academic and professional contexts. The chapters in the first unit of the book focus on relatively small pieces of discourse, and the chapters in the second unit of the book focus on large pieces of discourse that may include lengthy individual presentations. All of the chapters emphasize interaction, either one-on-one or one-to-a-group.

We make the following suggestions for the most effective use of the text.

1. Chapter sequence. Consider using the chapters sequentially. If you choose to omit one or more of the chapters based on your class size or the length of the instructional term, maintain the sequence that remains, as the later chapters integrate and assume competence with strategies presented in earlier chapters.

2. Introductory material. Read and discuss the chapter contents before proceeding with the activities. Highlight the interaction patterns described; note the grammatical patterns and explain them if necessary; define terms; and provide additional examples if you feel that they are needed. In short, do not pass casually over this part of the lesson. Make sure that students have a thorough introduction before they are asked to do the chapter activities.

3. Useful Expressions. Review and discuss the *Useful Expressions* with your students. Can they recognize any of them? Have they used any? Are there others that they have heard or used? What are the social parameters that would determine the use of the expressions? Discuss the notion that these expressions are to provide them with options and choices for use. They should be able to interpret all of the expressions, but they should be asked to use only a few.

4. Activities. The focus of the text is on practice. Each chapter provides a range of activities designed to build competence in component skills, with the final activity being the most integrated.

- We feel strongly that the students will be unable to do the activities unless they have first had a thorough orientation to the material in the chapter.
- Based on time contraints or class proficiency level, you may decide not to do all the activities in a single chapter. We suggest that you make this decision only after reading through all the activities provided.
- These activities are designed for maximum flexibility. As you begin to work with the book, you will see that some of the activities can be extended over many class periods. You will need to make a judgment about this in relation to your students' needs as well as your curricular goals. Note that preparation for the activities may be done at home or in class, alone or collaboratively.
- For any single activity, we recommend that you limit the number of presentations given in front of the class. It can be very time consuming and boring if all students make all presentations from all chapters.

- The class discussion activities are very important. They bring into focus various cultural issues and subtleties of social interaction. Use them creatively and elaborate on them in response to your students' knowledge and experience.

Our final recommendation is to steer you away from imposing a standard of perfection on your students. The language that they use in the classroom will be just like the language they will hear outside of the classroom. It will contain disfluencies, hesitations, repetitions, word searches, interruptions, and so on. Expect these characteristics in your students' developing communicative competence and honor them.

—— Acknowledgments ——

We would like to acknowledge with gratitude the following persons who gave us assistance as we developed and completed this project: David Lee, our editor at Heinle & Heinle Publishers who worked closely with us on the writing and production phases of the text, and who provided us with the direction and guidance this type of project needs; Peter Gaum, who helped bring a single integrated focus to the text; Patricia Kemp, who used parts of the text in her class; the following reviewers for their comments on the manuscript in its development: Pat Byrd, Alice Lyons-Quinn, Lynn Poirier, and Shelley Scammel; and Alexander and Steve, who entertained and encouraged us along the way. Finally, we extend a special kind of thanks to each other for the mutual inspiration and for the unique kind of experience we enjoyed while working together.

JANET L. KAYFETZ
MICHAELE E.F. SMITH

1

Strategies for Interacting One-On-One

1

Introducing Yourself and Others

What Will You Do in This Chapter?

In this chapter you will practice introducing yourself and introducing someone else in both formal and informal situations.

Why Is It Important to Be Able to Introduce Yourself and Others in a Variety of Situations?

It is important to be comfortable with self-introductions because you will often be asked to provide basic information about both your professional and personal backgrounds. You may be asked to introduce yourself not only to individuals, but also to classes, university committees, or even local clubs. You may also be expected to introduce your friends and colleagues to others as you socialize in groups and attend professional activities.

What Information Should You Include in a Self-Introduction?

The information you include in your introduction should be tailored to both the listener(s) and the specific situation. For example, it might be important for a university department committee to know the details of your research **goals**. This information, however, would not be appropriate in an introduction to a classmate, who would instead be interested in details about your personal background.

It is important to remember that the information you choose to include in your introduction will determine the kind of impression you make on your listeners.

How Should You Structure a Self-Introduction?

Following is the general structure of a self-introduction:

- your name
- general comments about your occupation or academic level if you are pursuing a degree
- additional professional or personal information appropriate to the specific context.

Examples of Self-Introductions

The following examples illustrate how a self-introduction will change depending on the particular context. Number 1 is an example of an *informal personal introduction*, number 2 is a *formal personal introduction* and number 3 is a *formal professional introduction*. Note the relationship between the specific context of each example and the specific information provided in the self-introduction.

1. This is an *informal personal introduction* given by a student to members of the International Students Club on a college campus.

   My name is Li Ning. I'm a junior, and I transferred here from the University of Taiwan. I've been here for three weeks and I'm working on my bachelor's degree in physics. I'm here because one of my friends came here and liked it a lot. I live in the dorm and I have an American roommate. I was homesick for the first two weeks, but now I'm getting used to the food and I'm making some friends.

2. This is an example of a *formal personal introduction* given by a businessman to an English class.

   My name is Hiroshi Seki. I'm from Tokyo and I'm a vice-president with Mitsubishi. In this position I have a lot of contact with our English-speaking business partners so the company has sent me here to study American English and culture. I'm enrolled in this program for nine months. When the program is finished my wife and my two children will join me and we'll travel for three months across the country. Right now I live with an American family here, and it not only helps my English but I'm enjoying the experience a lot.

3. This is a *formal professional introduction* given by a graduate student to the Organization of Women Graduate Students on a university campus.

My name is Maria del Rio and I'm from Spain. I'm in a doctoral program in chemical engineering and I'm one of three women in my program. Right now I'm working with Professor Pandey on two studies concerning oil and gas emulsion and their influence on the environment. The project is funded by a grant from an oil company. Ater I finish my degree I hope to do a post doc at the Environmental Institute at Boulder, Colorado. My long-term goal is to do research on environmental pollution in conjunction with government agencies in Spain.

── What Information Should You Include in an Introduction of Someone Else? ──

As with the self-introduction, the information you include in your introduction of another person should be appropriate to the listener(s) and the specific situation.

── How Should You Structure an Introduction of Another Person? ──

Following is the general structure of the introduction of another person:

- introductory phrase that identifies your relationship to the person you are introducing
- your name
- general comments about the person's occupation or interests
- additional comments that are appropriate to the specific context.

── Examples of Introductions of Other People ──

The following examples illustrate a range of types of introductions that you will be making. Number 1 provides examples of *informal personal* introductions of another person. Number 2 is an *informal professional* introduction of another person, and number 3 illustrates a *formal professional* introduction.

1. These are examples of *informal personal* introductions that might be given at a party.

   Sarah, this is my friend Dimitri. He's here visiting me from Belgium. We met when we went to school together in Ohio eight years ago.

   Tom, I want you to meet Patricia. She's my co-author. We actually met each other on a tour of museums in London six years ago and we kept in touch for a while and finally ended up doing a book together.

2. This is an example of an *informal professional* introduction of a colleague at a reception preceding a professional talk.

   Steve, I'd like to introduce my co-author Patricia Miller to you. We've been working together for about three years now. Besides working with me, she's a full professor at the University of London.

3. This is an example of a *formal professional* introduction given at a professional conference.

   I am pleased to have the chance to introduce to you my colleague Patricia Miller. Today she will be speaking on the subject of restoration of bronze artifacts. She brings a great deal of experience to this work, as she has been studying this area for the past eighteen years and has authored two major books on the subject. Patricia will be happy to answer any questions you may have at the end of her talk. Let's welcome Patricia Miller.

 — Sample Expressions for Self-Introductions

My name is _____ .

I'm from _____ .

I just arrived from _____ .

I'm a(n) _____ .
      researcher in biology.
      computer engineer.
      journalist.
      anthropologist.
      businessman.

(continued)

I'm a _____

      freshman.

      graduate student.

I'm here to study English.

I'm an undergraduate majoring in _____

      business economics.

      chemistry.

      art.

I'm a graduate student in _____

      educational psychology.

      physics.

      electrical and computer engineering.

I'm working on my bachelor's degree in psychology.

I'm working on a master's degree.

I'm in a master's program.

I'm working on a Ph.D.

I'm in a doctoral program.

I'm not enrolled in a degree program.

I'm studying _____

      second language acquisition.

      electromagnetism.

      software design.

      robotics.

I got interested in this field in high school.

I've always been interested in _____ .

I hope to finish my degree _____

      this year.

      in two years.

(continued)

I'm working with _____

    Professor Leslie Gordon on age differences in language acquisition.

    Professor Steven Edwards on electromagnetic radiation.

    Dr. Carrie Bridge on computer authoring languages.

Right now I'm working with a group on a state-funded project.

 **— Sample Expressions
for Introducing Another Person** ————————

This is my friend _____ .

I want you to meet _____ .

I am pleased to introduce _____ .

It gives me pleasure to introduce _____ .

This is _____ .

She's from _____ .

She's a(n) _____

        art history professor at London University.

        journalist.

        consultant.

        computer engineer.

She's working on _____ .

        her second book.

        a major research project.

        a major contract with a company in Brazil.

She will be happy to answer any questions you have after her talk.

She'll take questions after her presentation.

So let's welcome _____ .

Assignments

Assignment 1: Modifying Self-Introductions

The purpose of this activity is to practice modifying a self-introduction for a particular context. You will rewrite the examples of self-introductions on pp. 2–3 for levels of formality. Remember that the information you include in these new self-introductions should be tailored to both the listener(s) and the specific situation. Use Worksheet 1.

1. Example number 2 on pp. 2–3 is a *formal personal introduction* given by Hiroshi Seki. Assume the role of Mr. Seki and rewrite this self-introduction for

   a. an *informal personal* situation and

   b. a *formal professional* situation.

   You must use the biographical information given in the sample introduction and you will probably need to add additional information that is appropriate to the role.

2. Example number 3 on p. 3 is a *formal professional introduction* given by Maria del Rio. Assume the role of Ms. del Rio and rewrite this self-introduction for

   a. an *informal personal* situation and

   b. a *formal personal* situation.

   You must use the biographical information given in the sample introduction and you will probably need to add additional information that is appropriate to the role.

Assignment 2: Introducing Yourself

1. Write out an introduction of yourself using Worksheet 2.
   Refer to the examples of self-introductions on pp. 2–3 and use the sample expressions on pp. 4–5. Include the following information in your self-introduction:

   - Your name
   - Your home country
   - (If you are a student) Your year in school, your major, and your expected graduation date
     (If you are not a student) Your profession and the name of your employer
   - Three interesting details about yourself that you want your classmates to know

2. Practice your self-introduction with a partner.

Assignment 3: Introducing Another Person at an Informal Professional Gathering

For this activity, you will assume that the context for the introduction will be an *informal professional* gathering.

1. Your teacher will assign you a new partner for this activity. Find out information about your new partner so that you can introduce her to the class. Record this information on Worksheet 3.

2. Write out the full introduction on the back of Worksheet 3 and check it with your instructor. Refer to the examples on pp. 3–4 and use expressions from those provided on pp. 3–6.

3. On your own, practice giving this introduction. You may want to consult your partner for the accuracy of the introduction.

4. Your teacher will ask you and your partner to work with two other people. Each member of this new group will introduce her partner to the others.

Assignment 4: Introducing Another Person at a Formal Professional Meeting: Roleplay

For this activity, you will assume that the context for the introduction will be a *formal professional* meeting.

1. You will now work with a new partner. Each of you will assume the role of a professional whose background you create together.

2. Use Worksheet 4 to create a profile of your newly created role. Write out a *formal introduction* of your partner in her new role on the back of Worksheet 4.

3. Practice making your formal introduction with your partner.

4. **Class Activity**. Each person will be asked to introduce her partner to the rest of the class. Remember that your class is acting as the audience at a professional meeting where your partner will be presenting a talk.

Worksheet 1:
Modifying Self-Introductions

Directions: Use this worksheet to modify the self-introductions given in the examples on pp. 2–3. Use complete sentences. Refer to the sample introductions on pp. 2–3 and the sample expressions on pp. 4–6 to complete this worksheet.

Hiroshi Seki: Informal personal introduction

Identify the specific context:

_____

Hiroshi Seki: Formal professional introduction

Identify the specific context:

_____

Maria del Rio: Informal personal introduction

Identify the specific context:

_____

Maria del Rio: Formal personal introduction

Identify the specific context:

_____

━━ **Worksheet 2: Introducing Yourself** ━━━━━━━

Directions: Use this worksheet to prepare your self-introduction. Use complete sentences. Refer to the sample introductions on pp. 2–3 and the sample expressions on pp. 4–6 to complete this worksheet.

Context:

To whom are you introducing yourself?

_____

In what specific context are you introducing yourself (a party, a club, a meeting, etc.)?

_____

Information for your introduction:

1. Your name

2. Your home country

3. (If you are a student) Your year in school, your major, and your expected graduation date

   (If you are not a student) Your profession and the name of your employer

4. Three interesting details about yourself that are appropriate to your audience

   A.

   B.

   C.

Use the other side of this page to write out your complete self-introduction.

Write out the full self-introduction in the space below.

Worksheet 3: Introducing Another Person: Informal Professional Context

Directions: Use this worksheet to prepare an introduction of your partner. Use complete sentences. Refer to the examples of introductions of others on pp. 3–4 and the expressions provided on pp. 4–6 to complete this worksheet.

Context: An informal professional gathering.
Identify the specific type of gathering:

_____

Information for your introduction:

1. Your relationship to your partner

2. Your partner's name

3. General comments about your partner's occupation or interests

4. Additional comments appropriate to this context

Write out the full introduction in the space below.

— Worksheet 4: Introducing Another Person: Formal Professional Context —

Directions: Use this worksheet to prepare an introduction of your partner in her new role. Use complete sentences. Refer to the examples of introductions of others on pp. 3–4 and the expressions provided on pp. 4–6 to complete this worksheet.

Context: A formal professional gathering.
Identify the specific type of gathering:

_____

Information for your introduction:

1. Your relationship to the person you are introducing (panel moderator, colleague, friend, etc.)

2. Your partner's name

3. General comments about your partner's occupation or interests

4. Additional comments appropriate to this context

Write out the full introduction in the space below.

2

Asking Questions and Reformulating Questions

—— What Will You Do in This Chapter? ——————

In this chapter you will practice a technique for asking different kinds of questions. This technique involves asking a question and then re-asking it in a new way in case your listener did not understand the original question.

—— Why Is It Important to Be Able to Ask the Same Question in Different Ways? ——————

It is important to be able to reformulate questions to make them more precise because even the simplest questions are often misinterpreted or misunderstood.

—— What Kinds of Questions Will You Practice in This Chapter? ——————

In this chapter you will practice asking three kinds of questions:

■ questions that ask for information

- questions that ask for clarification
- questions that ask for an opinion

Following are examples of these three types of questions. Note that it is possible to use different grammatical forms for each type of question. Also note that in some cases the actual question is preceded by a statement.

1. **Asking for information:**
   - What hours is this office open?
   - Where do I buy a startup disk for the computer lab?

2. **Asking for clarification:**
   - Is the assignment supposed to be two typewritten pages or three?
   - I heard that the office isn't open during lunchtime, but it was open at lunch all last week. Have the official hours been changed?

3. **Asking for an opinion:**
   - In your opinion, does the International Students' office meet the needs of the students?
   - What do you think of Processquick hard drives?

── Reformulating Questions ──────────

Often when you ask a question, the response given by the listener is incomplete or even off the topic. This may happen because you have not formed the question clearly. It may also happen because the listener misunderstands the question, avoids the question, or redirects the question. In many cases, then, it may be necessary to ask the same question in a new way to refocus the listener on the meaning of your original question.

Use the following guidelines when reformulating questions:

- Be sure that the reformulated question is on the same topic as the original question.
- Use synonyms for the important words.
- Use a different grammatical construction in the new question.

Following are examples of an original question with two reformulations. Note that many of the reformulated questions are statements (called indirect questions) and not direct questions. Your teacher will discuss the grammatical constructions and synonyms used in each set of questions.

1. **Asking for information:**

   Original question: Where do I buy a startup disk for the computer lab?

   Reformulated question: Can you tell me where I can purchase a startup disk for the computer lab?

   Reformulated question: I want to buy a startup disk but I don't know where to get one.

2. **Asking for clarification:**

   Original question: Is the assignment supposed to be two typewritten pages or three?

   Reformulated question: Do you want us to hand in two or three typewritten pages?

   Reformulated question: I wanted to know if the paper should be two or three typewritten pages.

3. **Asking for an opinion:**

   Original question: In your opinion, does the International Students' office meet the needs of the students?

   Reformulated question: Do you think that students are well-served by this program?

   Reformulated question: What do you think about the services provided by the International Students' Office?

 — Sample Expressions for Asking Questions ——————

■ **Asking for information:**

What _____ ?

Where do I _____ ?

When _____ ?

How _____ ?

Why _____ ?

I want to know _____ .

(continued)

- **Asking for clarification:**

  Is the assignment supposed to be _____?

  I heard that _____ . Has anything been changed?

  I'm not sure whether _____ .

  The information I received said _____ . Is that correct?

  The letter I got said _____ . Could you confirm this?

- **Asking for an opinion:**

  In your opinion, _____?

  Don't you think that _____?

  What do you think of _____?

  Do you agree that _____?

- **Asking someone to repeat and checking for comprehension:**

  Could you repeat your question?

  Could you repeat that, please?

  Would you say that again?

  What did you say?

  What did you ask?

  What did you want to know?

  Did you just say _____?

  I didn't understand what you just said.

  I didn't catch that.

  I couldn't hear you.

  I didn't hear the last word.

Assignment 1: Asking Questions and Reformulating Them

The purpose of this activity is for you to practice the technique of asking questions and reformulating these questions. You will work with a partner.

1. Select two of the topics from the list below.

2. Generate a list of phrases and words that are associated with each topic you have chosen. This list of phrases and words should be helpful not only when you write an original question, but also when you write a reformulation of the question.

   For example, if your topic was "gambling," a list of phrases and words might include:

bet on the horses	lose
the odds	go to the races
hit the jackpot	place your bet
make a bet	play the lottery
win	take a risk

3. For each topic you have chosen, you will write six questions. The six questions will be an original question and a reformulated question asking for information, an original question and a reformulated question asking for clarification, and an original question and a reformulated question asking for an opinion. Refer to the lists of phrases and words you have just come up with as you write these questions. Write the questions on Worksheet 1 and have your teacher check them for grammar and vocabulary.

4. Roleplay asking these questions with your partner. Follow the dialogue format below.

   Speaker A asks the original question:
   ■ "I heard that the office is closed during lunchtime. Is that right?"

   Speaker B says:
   ■ "I'm sorry, I didn't understand your question."

   Speaker A reformulates the question:
   ■ "Did you say that the office is closed at lunchtime?"

Topics for Assignment number 1:

   dating customs

   attitudes toward energy use

   opportunities for higher education

family finances
gambling
economic conditions
political climate
attitudes toward television
censorship of the media
religious attitudes
immigrant populations
care of the elderly
treatment of mental health conditions
attitudes toward women
attitudes toward children
use of advanced technology in business
nuclear arms buildup or disarmament
use of nuclear power

Assignment 2: Getting Information by Asking Questions

In this assignment you will get information from native speakers of English on the topics you prepared in Assignment 1. This activity may be completed during class time or as a homework assignment.

Using the questions you wrote on Worksheet 1, get information about your topics from two native speakers of English.

- Tell the native speaker that this is an activity for one of your classes and that it will require only two or three minutes of her time.
- Be sensitive to your listener's responses. If you find that she has not understood your original question, use the reformulated question. Use Worksheet 1 as your guide.

Assignment 3: Class Discussion on Asking Questions and Reformulating Questions

Complete Worksheet 2 in preparation for a class discussion on the technique of using questions and reformulated questions.

── Worksheet 1:
Questions for Assignment 1 ────────

Directions: Write two forms of each question you will use in this activity. Remember that both questions should have the same content but should use different language.

Example:

Original question: Do you think students appreciate the services you offer?

Reformulated question: Do students seem to like the services provided by your office?

Topic 1 ─────────────────────────

1. **Asking for information**

   Original Question:

   Reformulated Question:

2. **Asking for clarification**

   Original Question:

   Reformulated Question:

3. **Asking for an opinion**

   Original Question:

   Reformulated Question:

(Use the back of this sheet for Topic 2)

1. **Asking for information**

   Original Question:

   Reformulated Question:

2. **Asking for clarification**

   Original Question:

   Reformulated Question:

3. **Asking for an opinion**

   Original Question:

   Reformulated Question:

Worksheet 2: Preparation for Class Discussion on Asking Questions and Reformulating Questions

Directions: Write brief answers to the following questions.

1. How did the interview with the native speaker go?

2. Did you get the response that you were looking for the first time you asked a question, or did you have to reformulate and ask it a second time? If you did have to reformulate the question, did the listener understand it and provide you with the information that you were looking for?

3. How did you know when the listener understood what you wanted to know?

4. How did you know when the listener did not understand your question? What did the listener say that indicated that she was not understanding you?

3

Making a Request and Granting a Request

── What Will You Do in This Chapter? ──────

In this chapter you will learn how to structure a request and how to follow through when it is granted.

── What Kinds of Requests Will You Practice? ──────

You will practice making requests that are frequently made in an academic setting such as a request for an exception to a university policy, a request for an extension of a deadline, and a request for financial support.

── What Is the Structure of a Request? ──────

A request is usually thought of as consisting of two "turns," a request turn and a response turn:

> **Turn 1**
> *Request:* I would like to request an extension on the due date for this project so that I have time to get the materials that I need.
>
> **Turn 2**
> *Response:* I don't see a problem with that. Why don't you take an extra week to find the materials you need? I'll expect your completed project on the last day of the quarter.

The request turn and response turn actually occur within a more complex conversational unit. To make it easier to understand, this *request conversational unit* will be divided into three sections:

1. **Opening the interaction.**

   In this part of the request conversational unit, the interaction is opened when the speaker introduces herself and makes a preliminary request for the listener's time. If the listener responds by saying that she is not available, then the speaker initiates a request for an appointment at a more convenient time and closes the conversation. If the listener is available, then the speaker continues by specifying her topic and giving the important information concerning her problem.

2. **Making the request and obtaining the response.**

   The speaker proceeds with the interaction by making her request and listening to the response. In this chapter, the focus will be on practicing requests that are granted. The next chapter will look at how to proceed when a request is denied.

3. **Closing the interaction.**

   In this section of the *request conversational unit*, the speaker brings the conversation to a close by expressing her appreciation for the listener's time and help.

Remember that each of these sections is a *series* of turns between the speakers.

—— Example of a Request Conversational Unit ——

Following is an example of how to prepare a request for an extension of a deadline.

1. Opening the Interaction

■ *Introduce yourself.*

"I'm Marcello Pelligrini, and I'm in your History of Science class."

■ *Make a polite request for your listener's time.**

"I just need a few minutes of your time to talk to you about my project."

If the listener is not available at the moment, then

■ *Arrange an appointment for a more convenient time.*

"Could I make an appointment to speak with you at a more convenient time?"

* Important note: *Do not* continue with your request if the listener has told you she is not available. It is considered extremely impolite to impose on someone else's time and will work against a positive outcome. On meeting with the listener at the arranged time, identify yourself again if necessary and proceed with the description of your situation as described above.

If the listener indicates that she has time to speak with you, then

■ *Specify the topic of the conversation.*

"What I would like to talk to you about concerns a problem that I'm having with meeting the final deadline for the project."

■ *Give the important information concerning your problem.*

"My topic is cross-cultural communication and I've been having problems getting the books I need from the library. The library doesn't have a large selection, and many of the books it does have seem to be on loan to professors and cannot be recalled."

2. Making the Request

■ *Make your request.*

Your request: "I would like to request an extension of the due date for this project so that I have time to get the materials I need."

■ *Listen to the response.*

Listener's response: "I don't see a problem with that. Why don't you take an extra week to find the materials you need? I'll expect your completed project on the last day of the quarter."

3. Closing the Interaction

■ *Express your appreciation for the listener's time and help.*

"Thank you for taking the time to help me with this."

Following is the complete example of the request for an extension of a deadline outlined above.

I'm Marcello Pelligrini, and I'm in your History of Science class. I just need a few minutes of your time to talk to you about my project. What I would like to talk to you about concerns a problem that I'm having with meeting the final deadline for the project. My topic is cross-cultural communication and I've been having problems getting the books I need from the library. The library doesn't have a large selection, and many of the books it does have seem to be on loan to professors and cannot be recalled.

Speaker's request: I would like to request an extension of the due date for this project so that I have time to get the materials I need.

Listener's response: I don't see a problem with that. Why don't you take an extra week to find the materials you need? I'll expect your completed project on the last day of the quarter.

Speaker: Thank you for taking the time to help me with this.

The example above outlines the course of action taken when you make a request and it is granted. What can you do if you make a request and it is not granted? See Chapter 4.

 — Sample Expressions for the Person Making the Request —————

- **Introducing Yourself**

  I'm Sandra Lee, a student in your computer class.
  My name is Jeff Brandt and I'm a second semester Freshman.

- **Requesting the Listener's Time**

  I just need a few minutes of your time.
  This will just take a few minutes.
  I won't take up too much of your time.
  I know you're very busy, so I'll try to be brief.

- **Introducing the Topic**

  I need to talk to you about _____ .

  What I would like to talk to you about concerns _____ .

  (continued)

The reason I asked to meet with you is to discuss _____ .

I want to discuss _____ .

I'd like your support for _____ .

I'm applying to _____ and I'd like to ask you if you would

_____ .

■ **Making Your Request**

I would like to request _____ .

I request that you _____ .

With your permission, I want to _____ .

I am requesting that you _____ .

Would it be possible for you to _____ ?

Would it be possible for me to _____ ?

■ **Terminating the Interaction**

Thank you for your help.

Thank you for meeting with me today.

I appreciate your willingness to help me.

■ **Requesting a New Appointment**

Since you're not available to meet with me now, could we arrange
another meeting time?

When would be a convenient time to discuss this?

Could I make an appointment to speak with you at a more convenient
time?

Sample Expressions for the Person Who Will Be Evaluating the Request

■ **Indicating That She Is Not Available**

I'm sorry, but I don't have any time right now.

I'm awfully busy right now.

Sorry, I'm in the middle of some very important work right now.

I can't talk with you now.

■ **Indicating That She Is Available**

Sure, come on in.

How can I help you?

I'm in the middle of something, but I can give you five minutes.

Yes, but no more than five minutes because I have a meeting to go to.

■ **Granting the Request**

I don't see a problem with that.

That'll be fine.

That should be no problem.

I don't want to make a habit of this, but in this particular case it will be okay.

Assignments

Assignment 1: Preparation of Roleplays

In this activity you will write out the sentences you will use to make requests. Follow the directions on Worksheets 1 and 2.

1. Below are situations for roleplays. Select two of these situations.

2. Using the example on p. 32, write out the requests you would make in each of the situations you have selected. Refer to the sample expressions on pp. 30–32.

3. Have your teacher go over your completed worksheets.

Situations for Roleplays

Request that your landlord	release you from a housing contract before the contract is over.
Request that your instructor	write a letter of recommendation for you.
Persuade your instructor to	give you an A minus instead of a B plus.
Persuade your instructor to	let you withdraw from his class.
Persuade your instructor to	let you come to class fifteen minutes late on a regular basis.
Persuade your instructor to	let you into her class. It is the second week of the quarter.
Persuade your advisor to	support your application for a leave of absence for the following quarter.
Persuade your department chair to	recommend you for the one TAship available.
Persuade the Director of Admissions	to waive an admissions requirement.
Convince your professor to	give you a week extension on your project when she has categorically stated that there will be none.
Convince your instructor to	allow you to take the final examination early/late.
Convince the librarian	to waive a late fine.

Assignment 2: Roleplaying Requests

In this activity you will work with a partner and roleplay the two situations you prepared in Assignment 1.

1. With your partner, roleplay the situation you prepared on Worksheet 1. Your partner will take the role of the listener. Remember that there are two conditions, one in which the listener is not available and the second in which the listener is available. Use your notes from Worksheet 1. Then switch roles, so that you take the role of the listener, and your partner makes the request.

2. Your teacher will ask you and your partner to work with another pair. Each pair will now roleplay their requests from Worksheet 2 while the other pair listens. The pair that is listening will evaluate the roleplays it observes using Worksheets 3 and 4.

3. Your teacher will assign you a new partner and a new situation to roleplay in front of the class.

Assignment 3: Class Discussion on Making Requests

Complete Worksheet 5 in preparation for a class discussion on requests.

— Worksheet 1: Preparation of Roleplay 1: Making a Request

Directions: Write sentences that you will use when you make your request and respond to your listener. Use appropriate sample expressions from pp. 30–32.

Situation 1: (requesting a letter of recommendation from a professor, requesting that your landlord release you from your contract, etc.)

_____

_____

Part One.   Roleplay: The Listener Is Not Available

Write complete sentences below.

■ Self-introduction:

■ Preliminary request for your listener's time:

■ *Listener's response indicating that she is not available:*

■ Request for an appointment at a more convenient time:

■ *Listener's response:*

■ Termination:

Part Two. Roleplay: Making a Request When the Listener Is Available

Write complete sentences below.

■ Self-introduction:

■ Preliminary request for your listener's time:

■ *Listener's response indicating that she is available:*

■ The topic:

■ The important information concerning your request:

■ The specific request:

Reformulation of the request in case the listener does not understand it the first time:

■ *Listener's response indicating that she will grant the request:*

■ Termination:

Worksheet 2: Preparation of Roleplay 2: Making a Request

Directions: Write sentences that you will use when you make your request and respond to your listener. Use appropriate sample expressions from pp. 30–32.

Situation 2: (requesting a letter of recommendation from a professor, requesting that your landlord release you from your contract, etc.)

_____

_____

Part One.   Roleplay: The Listener Is Not Available

Write complete sentences below.

■ Self-introduction:

■ Preliminary request for your listener's time:

■ *Listener's response indicating that she is not available:*

■ Request for an appointment at a more convenient time:

■ *Listener's response:*

■ Termination:

Part Two.   Roleplay: Making a Request When the Listener Is Available

Write complete sentences below.

■ Self-introduction:

■ Preliminary request for your listener's time:

■ *Listener's response indicating that she is available:*

■ The topic:

■ The important information concerning your request:

■ The specific request:

Reformulation of the request in case the listener does not understand it the first time:

■ *Listener's response indicating that she will grant the request:*

■ Termination:

Worksheet 3:
   Evaluation of Roleplays

Directions: Answer the questions below so that you can offer helpful suggestions to the person you are evaluating.

Situation: (Write the situation that you are evaluating below.)

---

1. Was the self-introduction and request for the listener's time brief and cordial?

2. Was the problem clearly presented?

3. Was the request direct and clearly stated?

4. Was the interaction terminated appropriately?

5. What two things could your classmate change to improve making her requests?

Worksheet 4:
Evaluation of Roleplays

Directions: Answer the questions below so that you can offer helpful suggestions to the person you are evaluating.

Situation: (Write the situation that you are evaluating below.)

_____

_____

1. Was the self-introduction and request for the listener's time brief and cordial?

2. Was the problem clearly presented?

3. Was the request direct and clearly stated?

4. Was the interaction terminated appropriately?

5. What two things could your classmate change to improve making her requests?

**Worksheet 5: Discussion of Issues
Around Making a Request**

Directions: Complete this worksheet before the class discussion. Be prepared to offer your comments.

1. Why do you ask for someone's time when making a request?

2. What do due dates and deadlines really mean?

3. What are the consequences of continuing the interaction after the speaker has indicated that she is not available to speak with you? What are the possible interpretations of your behavior?

4. Go over the expressions used when making a request on pp. 30–32. Discuss the level of formality, style, and tone of each.

4

Making a Request, Denying a Request, and Negotiating a Compromise

---

—— What Will You Do in This Chapter? ——

The previous chapter describes how to make a request and how to follow through when it is granted. But not all requests are granted. In this chapter you will practice how to negotiate when your request is denied.

—— What Do You Do When You Make a Request and It Is Denied? ——

There are two options for you if your request is turned down. (1) You can choose to end the discussion or (2) you can try to negotiate a compromise. The listener's responses will help you determine which course of action is the appropriate one.

1. **How do you end the interaction when your request has been firmly denied?**

If you have determined that the listener will not grant your request, thank her for her time and leave. You will know that your request has been firmly denied because denials of this type are often brief and direct.

Example 1: A Request and a Firm Denial

Your original request:	I would like to request an extension of the due date for this project so that I have time to get the materials that I need.
Firm denial:	I'm sorry, but that won't be possible. I want all papers on the due date.
You say:	Thank you for speaking with me. At least I had a chance to tell you my situation. I'll do my best.
Or you can say:	I'm sorry we couldn't work it out. Thank you for talking with me.

Example 2: A Request and a Firm Denial

Your original request:	Would it be possible to begin work on this project before we obtain the final approval?
Firm denial:	I'm sorry, but that goes against policy and we can make no exceptions.
You say:	But this delay will cost our investors quite a bit of money. Is there any way that this can be taken into consideration?
Denial:	I'm sorry, but that won't be possible.
You say:	Thank you for the information.

2. **Your request has been denied, but something in the listener's response makes you believe that she is willing to discuss an alternative. How can you negotiate a compromise to your original request?**

Denials that may be open to negotiation are often "softened" and not as brief as a firm denial. If you think that the listener is open to it, an appropriate course of action to take is to negotiate a compromise.

In negotiating a compromise, both speakers work together over a number of turns to reach an agreement. Often discussions of this type are longer than the example below.

Example 1: A Request and a "Softened" Denial

Your original request:	I would like to request an extension of the due date for this project so that I have time to get the materials that I need.

"Softened" denial:	I'm sorry, but that won't be possible. I was hoping to get all papers on the due date. I do not want to make any exceptions to this policy unless an individual case warrants it.
You say:	If that's not possible, could you help me work out another solution?
Listener says:	Well, I would prefer that you change your topic so that you can find materials easily and get me your project on time. Extending the due date is out of the question.
You say:	I did have another idea for a topic. Would a project on body language be acceptable?
Listener says:	That will be fine. Is there enough material available?
You say:	Yes, I've already found some references.
Listener says:	Good, then I'll expect your project on the original due date.
You say:	Thank you for helping me work this out.

Example 2: A Request and a "Softened" Denial

Your original request:	Would it be possible to give me credit on my transcript for the work I did this summer at a bank?
"Softened" denial:	We rarely grant credit for summer work. You can submit this form to the admissions committee and they will make a decision.
You say:	I have a letter that my supervisor wrote and it explains what my responsibilities were. Would you read it and tell me if you could make an exception in my case?
Listener says:	I can ask the admissions committee to read it along with your completed form and I can have an answer for you the beginning of next week.
You say:	Is there any way that you could give me an answer before next week?
Listener says:	No. The committee meets once a week and reports its decisions by Tuesday afternoon.
You say:	Thank you.
Listener says:	Good luck.

—— Sample Expressions for the Person
Making the Request ——————

■ **Making the request**

I would like to request ———————————————— .

I request that you ————————————————————— .

With your permission, I want to ————————————— .

I am requesting that you ————————————————— .

Would it be possible for you to ———————————— ?

Would it be possible for me to ————————————— ?

■ **Indicating that you are open to other solutions**

If this is not possible, do you have any suggestions that might help me?

If that's not satisfactory, do you know of another way to handle this?

■ **Proposing a compromise**

Well, I can get the outline done by then, but I know the paper won't be finished. Would that be acceptable?

If it's not possible to waive the exams, then the soonest I can take them is next Fall. Would that be possible?

 —— Sample Expressions for the Person
Who Will Be Evaluating the Request —————

■ **Giving a Firm Denial**

That's not possible.

I would like to help you, but ————————————— .

If I could, I would, but ————————————————— .

I have no jurisdiction over this.

Thank you for bringing it to my attention.

(continued)

- **Softening the denial to indicate that you may be open to alternatives**

  You know, all the other lab sections are full.

  You need to make a formal request in writing and send it to the committee.

  Before we can make that decision, we have to review the case.

  I don't like to do this because it sets a precedent.

  I'll have to look into this.

- **Compromising**

  This is unusual, but the committee feels that the circumstances warrant special consideration.

  Okay, but this is the only time we can make an exception.

  Well, we can't waive the requirement, but we can extend the due date for two weeks.

—— Assignments ——————————————

Assignment 1: Roleplaying the Negotiation of Denied Requests

In this assignment, you will work with a partner and create two roleplays in which a request is denied. In one of the roleplays you will be the person who makes the request and in the other roleplay you will be the person who denies the request.

1. Follow the directions on Worksheets 1 and 2 to prepare the roleplays.

2. Practice your requests and your responses with your partner using your notes from Worksheets 1 and 2. Be sure that you have the chance to practice each role. Remember that there are two conditions, one in which the listener gives a firm denial and the second in which the listener gives a softened denial.

Assignment 2: Presentation of a Roleplay for the Class

Your teacher will assign you a new partner and give you a new situation to roleplay in front of the class. This situation will be chosen from the list below. Your teacher will assign one of your classmates to evaluate the roleplay using Worksheet 3.

Request that your landlord	release you from a housing contract before the contract is over.
Request that your instructor	write a letter of recommendation for you.

Persuade your instructor to	give you an A minus instead of a B plus.
Persuade your instructor to	let you withdraw from his class.
Persuade your instructor to	let you come to class fifteen minutes late on a regular basis.
Persuade your instructor to	let you into her class. It is the second week of the quarter.
Persuade your advisor to	support your application for a leave of absence for the following quarter.
Persuade your department chair to	recommend you for the one TAship available.
Persuade the Director of Admissions	to waive an admissions requirement.
Convince your professor to	give you a week extension on your project when she has categorically stated that there will be none.
Convince your instructor to	allow you to take the final examination early/late.
Convince the librarian	to waive a late fine.

Assignment 3: Class Discussion

Use Worksheet 4 to prepare for a class discussion of some of the important issues regarding requests, denials, and negotiations.

—— **Worksheet 1: Preparation for Roleplay 1:**
       Making a Request and Having It Denied ————

Directions: Follow the instructions on this worksheet to prepare your role-play.

Check the role you are taking.

■ the person making the request (Speaker A) _____ .

■ the person responding to the request (Speaker B) _____ .

Describe Your Roleplay Situation

Create a situation in which a request is denied. The context should be formal and reflect interactions that are likely to occur in the academic, business, or professional communities.

■ What is the situation (professor's office, business office, a committee meeting)?

■ Who is Speaker A (student, secretary, business partner)?

■ Who is Speaker B (professor, business executive, university official)?

The Request   (Complete this section if you are Speaker A.)

Using the sample expressions on pp. 48–49, write sentences that you will use when making your request in the context you have specified above.

■ Introduce yourself and make a request for the listener's time:

■ The listener responds by indicating that she is available:

■ Introduce the topic:

■ Give the important information concerning your problem:

■ Make your request:

Respond to the Request   (Complete this section with your partner.)

Using the sample expressions on pp. 48–49 write out two dialogues with your partner. The first dialogue will be a **firm denial** followed by an appropriate closing remark. The second dialogue will be a **softened denial** followed by a negotiation sequence where you and your partner negotiate an alternative solution to the original request. Remember that negotiations can often be quite long. (Note: You may want to refer to the examples provided in this chapter.)

Dialogue 1: Firm Denial

Speaker A: (Request) _____

_____

Speaker B: (Firm denial) _____

_____

Speaker A: (Closing remarks) _____

_____

Speaker B: (Closing remarks) _____

_____

Dialogue 2: Softened Denial

Speaker A: (Request) _____

_____

Speaker B: (Softened denial) _____

_____

Speaker A: (Opening remark to the negotiation of a solution) _____

_____

_____

Complete the remainder of the negotiation dialogue below. Use as many turns as you need.

Speaker A: _____

_____

_____

Speaker B: _____

_____

_____

Speaker A: _____

_____

_____

Speaker B: _____

_____

_____

Worksheet 2: Preparation for Roleplay 2: Making a Request and Having It Denied

Directions: Follow the instructions on this worksheet to prepare your role-play.

Check the role you are taking.

■ the person making the request (Speaker A) _____ .

■ the person responding to the request (Speaker B) _____ .

Describe Your Roleplay Situation

Create a situation in which a request is denied. The context should be formal and reflect interactions that are likely to occur in the academic, business, or professional communities.

■ What is the situation (professor's office, business office, a committee meeting)?

■ Who is Speaker A (student, secretary, business partner)?

■ Who is Speaker B (professor, business executive, university official)?

The Request (Complete this section if you are Speaker A.)

Using the expressions on pp. 48–49, write sentences that you will use when making your request in the context you have specified above.

■ Introduce yourself and make a request for the listener's time:

■ The listener responds by indicating that she is available:

- Introduce the topic:

- Give the important information concerning your problem:

- Make your request:

Respond to the Request (Complete this section with your partner.)

Using the sample expressions on pp. 48–49, write out two dialogues with your partner. The first dialogue will be a **firm denial** followed by an appropriate closing remark. The second dialogue will be a **softened denial** followed by a negotiation sequence where you and your partner negotiate an alternative solution to the original request. Remember that negotiations can often be quite long. (Note: You may want to refer to the examples provided in this chapter.)

Dialogue 1: Firm Denial

Speaker A: (Request) _____

_____

Speaker B: (Firm denial) _____

_____

Speaker A: (Closing remarks) _____

_____

Speaker B: (Closing remarks) _____

_____

Dialogue 2: Softened Denial

Speaker A: (Request) _____

_____

Speaker B: (Softened denial) _____

_____

Worksheet 2 *(continued)*

Speaker A: (Opening remark to the negotiation of a solution) _____

_____

_____

Complete the remainder of the negotiation dialogue below. Use as many turns as you need.

Speaker A: _____

_____

_____

Speaker B: _____

_____

_____

Speaker A: _____

_____

_____

Speaker B: _____

_____

_____

Worksheet 3:
   Evaluation of Roleplays

Directions: Answer the questions below so that you can offer helpful suggestions to the pair you are evaluating.

Situation: (Write the situation that you are evaluating below.)

_____

_____

1. Was the self-introduction and request for the listener's time brief and cordial?

2. Was the problem clearly presented?

3. Was the request direct and clearly stated?

4. Was the denial appropriately "firm"?

   Was the denial appropriately "soft"?

5. Was the negotiation of the original request carried out effectively?

6. Was the interaction terminated appropriately?

(Please turn over and answer Question 7.)

7. What two things could your classmates change to improve their negotiating skills?

Worksheet 4: Discussion of Issues Concerning Requests That Have Been Denied

Directions: Write short answers for the following questions and be prepared to go over them with the class.

1. What is the difference between a request and a demand?

2. Statements are often used to make indirect requests. What is the hidden request in the following statement made by a student to a teacher?

   "I can't do this assignment."

   Why might the statement "I can't do this assignment." sound more like a challenge than a request? What should be added to this indirect request to make it less abrupt?

3. What are the consequences of trying to negotiate a compromise to your request after you have been given a firm denial?

4. Describe an example of a time when you made a request that was denied. Do you think you could have presented it in a different way to obtain a favorable outcome? Be ready to discuss your experience with the class.

C H A P T E R

5

Describing Objects and Processes Using Diagrams

—— What Will You Do in This Chapter? ——

In this chapter, you will practice describing objects and processes represented in diagrams.

—— Why Practice Describing Diagrams? ——

Speakers in professional and academic fields often use visual aids when presenting information. It is therefore important that you be able not only to present visual information but also to understand and interpret information that is presented visually.

—— What Is a Diagram? ——

A diagram is a drawing that represents an *object* or *process*. The drawing is carefully labeled and sometimes quite detailed. Diagrams are used to illustrate *objects* such as the human eye, the components of a computer, a plant cell, or a camera. Diagrams are also used to illustrate *processes* such as mitosis, evaporation, pollination, or crystallization.

── How Do You Interpret a Diagram? ────────

To give a clear description of a diagram, you must do the following:

- Specify the subject.
- Orient the audience.
- Specify the order of presentation.
- Point out the components labeled in the diagram.
- Begin your talk.

── Example 1: Description of an Object ────────

Figure 1 (p. 65) is a diagram of the human eye. Following is an example of how to prepare a description of this diagram.

1. **Specify the subject of the diagram with a clear statement.**

   "This is a diagram of the structure of the human eye."

2. **Orient the audience to the general layout of the diagram.**

   "As you can see, this is a diagram of a cross section of the human eye with the front of the eye on the left and the optic nerve on the right."

3. **Specify the order in which you will present the parts of the diagram. This order will vary according to the particular subject. Possible orders of presentation are top to bottom, bottom to top, outside to inside, inside to outside, left to right, right to left.**

   "I am going to describe the eye by beginning with the outer structure and moving to the inner structure. In this way we will end with the inner eye, the topic I wish to discuss at length."

4. **Point out the components labeled in the diagram. Follow the order that you have chosen.**

   "As you can see in the diagram, the outer structure of the human eye is called the encasement. Next to the encasement, and moving toward the center of the eye, is the retina. . . ."

5. **After you have pointed out all of the important components in the diagram, make the transition to the main body of your talk.**

   "Now that you have an orientation to the structure of the eye, I'd like to concentrate specifically on the inner eye. Please use the diagram as a reference while I'm speaking."

The complete description of Figure 1 reads as follows:

"This is a diagram of the structure of the human eye. As you can see, this is a diagram of a cross section of the human eye with the front of the eye on the left and the optic nerve on the right. I am going to describe the eye by beginning with the outer structure and moving to the inner structure. In this way we will end with the inner eye, the topic I wish to discuss at length. As you can see in the diagram, the outer structure of the human eye is called the encasement. Next to the encasement, and moving toward the center of the eye, is the retina. . . . Now that you have an orientation to the structure of the eye, I'd like to concentrate specifically on the inner eye. Please use the diagram as a reference while I'm speaking."

Figure 1. Structure of the human eye.

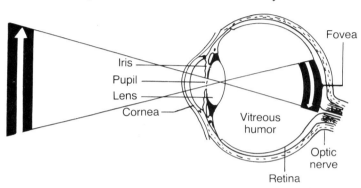

—— Example 2: Description of a Process ——————

Figure 2 (p. 66) is a simple diagram of the printing process. Following is an example of how to prepare a description of this diagram.

1. **Specify the subject of the diagram with a clear statement.**

   "Each of you has a diagram showing the printing process."

2. **Orient the audience to the general layout of the diagram.**

   "You can see the imprint block and the piece of paper, two essential elements in the printing process."

3. **Specify the order in which you will present the parts of the diagram. This order will vary according to the particular subject. Possible orders of presentation are top to bottom, bottom to top, outside to inside, inside to outside, left to right, right to left.**

   "I will work from left to right and describe the process that must be followed to print a figure using blocks and paper."

4. **Point out the components labeled in the diagram. Follow the order that you have chosen.**

"I will first describe the part of the diagram labeled number one, the imprint block, which is on the left of the page. The symbol to be printed is usually raised, as it is in the diagram. When ink is applied to the imprint block, the symbol is coated with ink and the outline is not. In the next step the printing medium is applied to the inked block, which is on the right of the diagram, labeled number 2. . . ."

5. **After you have pointed out all of the important components in the diagram, make the transition to the main body of your talk.**

"With this in mind, I would like to go back now and discuss a brief history of the development of the printing process."

The complete description of Figure 2 reads as follows:

"Each of you has a diagram showing the printing process. You can see the imprint block and the piece of paper, two essential elements in the printing process. I will work from left to right and describe the process that must be followed to print a figure using blocks and paper. I will first describe the part of the diagram labeled number one, the imprint block, which is on the left of the page. The symbol to be printed is usually raised, as it is in the diagram. When ink is applied to the imprint block, the symbol is coated with ink and the outline is not. In the next step the printing medium is applied to the inked block, which is on the right of the diagram, labeled number 2. . . . With this in mind, I would like to go back now and discuss a brief history of the development of the printing process."

Figure 2. The printing process. (1) Imprint block has raised or recessed characters; surface is wetted with ink. (2) Printing medium (paper) is applied to inked block for transferred imprint of characters.

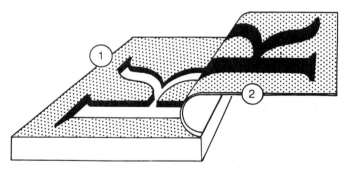

Specifying the Diagram

This is a diagram of _____ .

As you can see, this diagram shows the process of _____ .

Orienting the Audience to the General Layout of the Diagram

As you can see, this is a diagram of a cross section of the _____ .

In this diagram, you can see the _____ , an essential component
of this process.

Specifying the Order of Presentation of Information

I am going to work from the center outward in explaining this diagram.

Working from left to right, I will describe the process of _____ .

Starting from the top, you can see the sequence of the _____
process.

Identifying the Components of the Diagram

As you can see in the diagram, the _____ is called the _____ .

The square object in the center is the _____ .

Transitional Phrases

Now that you have an orientation to the parts of the _____ , I'd like to

concentrate specifically on the _____ .

Please use the diagram as a reference while I am speaking.

With this in mind, I would like to go back now and discuss _____ .

Locational Expressions

In the upper right-hand corner, there is _____ .

You will note the _____ in the lower left-hand corner.

(continued)

As you can see on the left, there is a structure shaped like a _____ .

This is the _____ .

If you start from the center and work out, you can see the _____ .

There is a line that runs down the middle of the diagram. To the left of this line, you will find _____ ; to the right of this line, you will find

_____ .

—— Assignments ——

Assignment 1: Preparing and Presenting a Description of a Diagram

In this activity, you will prepare a description of one of the diagrams from pp. 74–80 and practice it with a partner.

1. Select one of the diagrams on pp. 74–80.

2. Use Worksheet 1 to prepare a description of your diagram. Use the sample expressions on pp. 67–68. Practice giving this description at home.

3. Your teacher will assign you a partner. Present your description to your partner. Your partner will give you feedback on the clarity and accuracy of your description.

Assignment 2: Describing a Diagram from Your Field of Study

In this activity, you will prepare a description of a diagram you have chosen from your field of study or profession. After preparing a description of it, you will present your description to the class.

1. Select a diagram from your field of study. Make copies of this diagram for each member of the class.

2. Use Worksheet 2 to prepare a description of your diagram. Practice giving this description at home before presenting it to the class.

3. Present your description to the class. Your teacher will assign at least one of your classmates to give you feedback on your presentation using the feedback form on Worksheet 3.

Worksheet 1: Preparing a Description of a Diagram

Directions: Use the worksheet to prepare your description of a diagram. Use complete sentences.

Check the type of diagram you are describing:

object _____

process _____

1. Identify the diagram you have chosen from those provided on pp. 74–80.

2. State the subject of the diagram.

3. Orient the audience to the diagram.

4. State the order in which you will present the parts of the diagram.

5. Point out the components labeled in the diagram.

6. Write the phrase you will use to make the transition to the main body of your talk.

Worksheet 2: Describing a Diagram from Your Field of Study or Profession

Directions: Use this worksheet to prepare your description of the diagram you have selected. Use complete sentences.

Check the type of diagram you are describing:

object _____

process _____

1. State the subject of the diagram.

2. Orient the audience to the diagram.

3. State the order in which you will present the parts of the diagram.

4. Point out the components labeled in the diagram.

5. Write the phrase you will use to make the transition to the main body of your talk.

Worksheet 3: Describing a Diagram
Feedback Form

Directions: Complete this form for your partner. Rate the speaker on each point listed below by using the scale of 1 to 4.

Name of Speaker _____

Topic _____

Poor			Excellent
1	2	3	4

1. _____ The topic for the talk was stated clearly.

2. _____ The diagram was appropriate for the topic.

3. _____ The diagram was clearly labeled.

4. _____ The subject of the diagram was clearly stated.

5. _____ The orientation to the layout of the diagram was clearly stated.

6. _____ The order of presentation of the parts of the diagram was clearly stated.

7. _____ The labeled components in the diagram were clearly described.

8. _____ The transitional phrase to the main body of the talk was clear.

Figure 3. Maslow's hierarchy of needs.

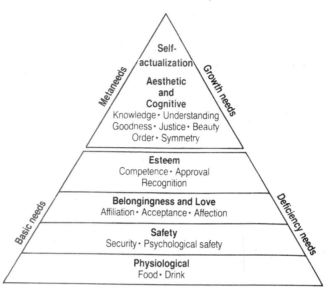

Figure 4. The basics of television broadcasting.

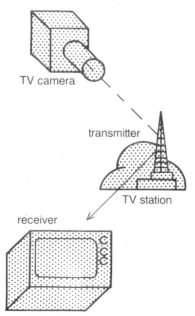

TV camera

transmitter

TV station

receiver

The TV camera is used to form an optical image. An electron beam registers lightness or darkness of the image into a picture.

The registered picture is converted to electrical signals that are amplified and transmitted by radio waves.

The TV set (receiver) reconstitutes the lightness or darkness code of the image, which is "painted" onto a phosphorous screen.

The scan of the electronic beam in the station's TV camera is so rapid that our eyes preceive an illusion of moving images.

Figure 5. The communications plaque from Pioneer X.

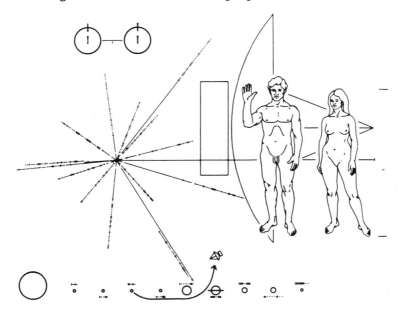

Figure 6. Gaze deviation of infants.

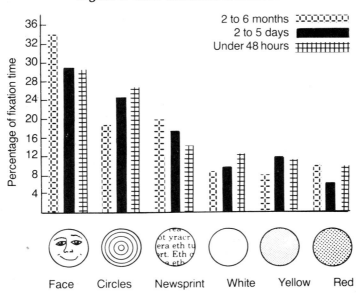

Figure 7. A typical cable television distribution system.

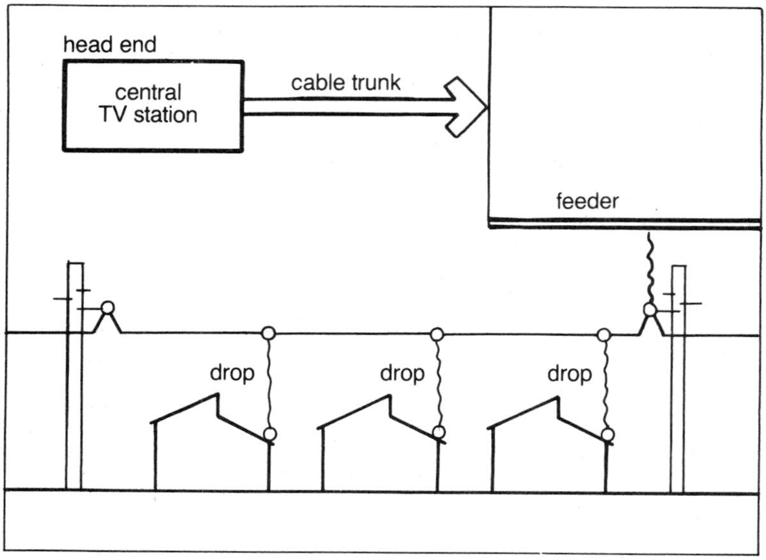

head end

central
TV station

cable trunk

feeder

drop

drop

drop

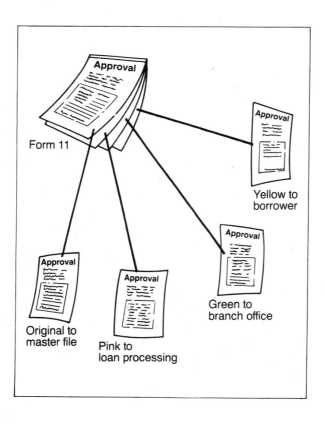

Form 11

Approval

Approval

Yellow to
borrower

Approval

Green to
branch office

Approval

Original to
master file

Approval

Pink to
loan processing

Figure 8. Flowchart of the routing of loan approval form 11.

Figure 9. The human brain at four stages of development, from three weeks after conception to birth.

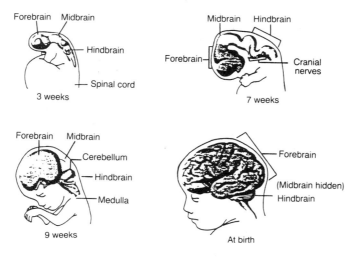

3 weeks

7 weeks

9 weeks

At birth

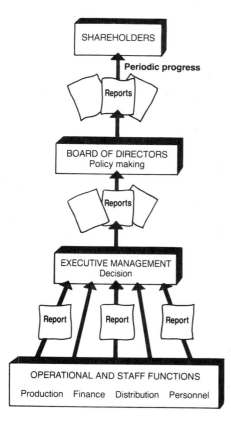

Figure 10. The general upward flow of reports.

Figure 11. Sex determination at fertilization. At the top of the figure are an ovum and four spermatozoa, two with the large X sex chromosome and two with the smaller Y sex chromosome. The ovum always contains only the X sex chromosome. (The sex chromosomes are outlined.) In (a) the zygote (fertilized egg) contains an X spermatozoon and will result in a girl. In (b) the zygote contains a Y spermatozoon and will therefore be a boy.

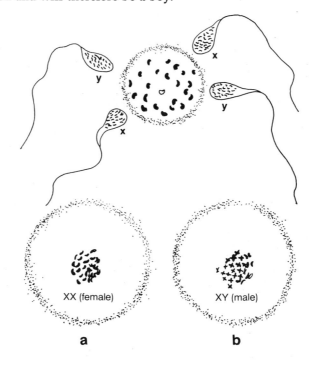

Figure 12. The family life cycle by length of time in years in each of eight stages. (From Duvall, 1977, p. 148. Based upon data from the U.S. Bureau of the Census and from the National Center for Health Statistics, Washington, D.C.)

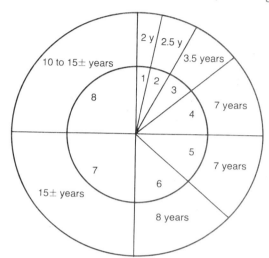

1. Married couples without children.

2. Childbearing families
   (oldest child birth-30 months)

3. Families with preschool children
   (oldest child 30 months-6 years)

4. Families with schoolchildren
   (oldest child 6-13 years)

5. Families with teenagers
   (oldest child 13-20 years)

6. Families launching young adults
   (first child gone to last child leaving home)

7. Middle-aged parents
   (empty nest to retirement)

8. Aging family members
   (retirement to death of both spouses)

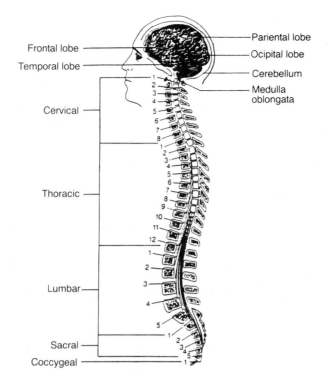

Figure 13. The central nervous system of an adult.

Figure 14. Slavery in the United States (1821).

Strategies for Structuring Information for Presentation

C H A P T E R

6

Presenting a
Verbal Summary

---— **What Will You Do in This Chapter?** ————————

In this chapter you will practice giving verbal summaries of short reading passages.

---— **Why Practice Giving Verbal Summaries?** ——————

The ability to give verbal summaries of information that you have read is a fundamental skill of academic interaction. Although this chapter will not focus on practicing written summaries, practicing verbal summaries will enhance this related skill.

---— **What Is a Summary?** ————————————

A summary is a shortened version of a more detailed body of information. A good summary expresses clearly, concisely, and accurately the essence of the original. While a summary is expected to include all the important ideas from the original, it must do this in fewer words.

How Is a Verbal Summary Structured?

In general, most talks have three sections: an opening, a body, and a termination. This structure is recommended to help you organize what you are going to say.

- **Opening:** The *opening* frames your comments and provides a context for them. In a summary of a reading, the opening often states the title and author(s) of the reading, the section(s) that will be summarized if appropriate, as well as a concise statement of the general topic discussed in the reading.
- **Body:** The *body* summarizes the main points discussed in the reading and may include examples taken from the text. This section also reports the author(s)' position or point of view if appropriate.
- **Termination:** The *termination* concludes your comments.

Examples of Summaries Based on This Structure

The following are examples of the opening–body–termination structure described above. Note that each summary has a different focus.

1. The focus of this summary is on definitions of terms given in an article.

   (**Opening**) The first section of the article addresses basic definitions used throughout the discussion. (**Body**) The three terms that the author defines are affect, input, and cognition. Affect is . . . Input is defined as . . . The third definition is cognition, which the author says is . . . (**Termination**) Other sections of the article continue the discussion of these terms to show how they can be integrated into a model of language acquisition.

2. The focus of this summary is on the point of view of the author of an article.

   (**Opening**) The middle section of this article is very important because this is where the author states her point of view. (**Body**) The author's point of view is that language acquisition is a natural developmental process. She supports this position with research from the fields of child development, psycholinguistics, and physiology. One example she cites from the field of child development is . . . . An example from the research in psycholinguistics is . . . . (**Termination**) Finally, an example from physiology cited by the author is . . . .

3. The focus of this summary is on a description of a research project.

   (**Opening**) I have chosen to summarize an article by Steven P. Simon, titled *Barnacle Colonies on the Santa Barbara Pier*. In this article, Simon discusses his research on the changes these colonies have undergone in the past decade.

(Body) According to Simon, there are two factors that influence the evolution of these colonies. First, there is _____ . Second, there is _____ . His best example illustrating this evolution is _____ . The author's point of view is that _____ . **(Termination)** Simon concludes by saying . . . .

What Should You *Not* Do in a Verbal Summary?

- Do not read aloud from the original text. Use your own words.
- Do not express your own point of view. Give an accurate report of the discussion presented by the author(s).
- Do not spend any time discussing minor points from the reading. Stay focused on the major point(s).
- Do not speak for too long.

Sample Expressions for Presenting a Verbal Summary

> ### ■ Giving the Title of the Article and the Author(s)
>
> The article I would like to summarize is written by _____ and is titled _____ .
>
> The section of the text I have been asked to summarize is the section on _____ , titled _____ .
>
> I have chosen to summarize an article by _____ , called _____ .
>
> ### ■ Giving a Concise Statement of the General Topic Discussed in the Article
>
> What _____ says is that _____ .
>
> The point of this article is to explain _____ .
>
> *(continued)*

In this article, (the author) _____

reviews the subject of _____ .

In this article, (the author) _____

says _____ .

■ Choosing the Most Important Ideas and Examples from the Article

The author emphasizes that _____ .

The author argues that _____ .

The author has examined three approaches to _____ .

The first is _____ .

The second is _____ .

The third is _____ .

There are two main characteristics that need to be understood:

first, there is _____ ,

and second, there is _____ .

An example that explains this clearly is _____ .

The author's best example of this is _____ .

■ Reporting the Author's Position or Point of View if Appropriate

The author's point of view is that _____ .

According to the author, _____ .

It is clear that the author favors _____ .

The author found that _____ .

The author concludes that _____ .

─── Assignments ───

Assignment 1: Summarizing a Short Reading

The purpose of this activity is to practice the strategy of preparing an accurate verbal summary of a short reading. You will work with a partner, and together you will prepare a summary of one of the readings at the end of the chapter. Use Worksheet 1.

1. As a pair, select and read one of the readings on pp. 95 through pp. 110. Complete Worksheet 1 to prepare your summary of this reading. Use the sample expressions on pp. 83–84.

2. For practice, each of you should give the verbal summary to your partner. The presentation of your summary should take no longer than two minutes.

Assignment 2: Summarizing a Short Reading from Your Field of Study or Profession

In this activity, you will present a summary of a short reading from your field of study or profession. After preparing your summary, you will practice giving it to a partner and then present it to the entire class. Your summary should be no more than four minutes.

1. Select a short reading from your field of study and use Worksheet 2 to prepare a summary of it.

2. Practice your summary at home.

3. Present the summary you have prepared to a classmate. Your partner will give you feedback on your summary using the feedback form on Worksheet 3.

4. Present your summary to the class. Your teacher will assign a class member to give you feedback on your summary using Worksheet 4.

Worksheet 1:
Summary of a Short Reading

Directions: Use this worksheet to prepare a summary of one of the readings from the chapter. Use the back of this page if you need more space.

Title of passage: _____

1. **Opening**   (Give the title and author and state the main idea discussed in the reading.)

2. **Body**   (Mention the main points and important supporting examples; state clearly and concisely the author's point of view or attitude.)

3. **Termination**   (Conclude your remarks here.)

— **Worksheet 2: Summary of a
Short Reading from Your Field** —————

Directions: Use this worksheet to prepare a summary of a reading you have chosen from your field. Use the back of this page if you need more space.

Title of passage: _____

1. **Opening**   (Give the title and author and state the main idea discussed in the reading.)

2. **Body**   (Mention the main points and important supporting examples; state clearly and concisely the author's point of view or attitude.)

3. **Termination**   (Conclude your remarks here.)

Worksheet 3: Summary Feedback Form for Partner

Directions: Complete this form for your partner.

Name of Speaker _____

Topic _____

A. Rate the speaker on each point listed below by using the scale of 1 to 4.

Poor 1	2	3	Excellent 4

1. _____ The title and author were clearly stated at the beginning.

2. _____ The topic of the reading was stated clearly and concisely.

3. _____ The examples chosen clearly supported their respective points.

4. _____ The speaker's pronunciation was clear and evenly paced.

B. Check the items below that apply to the speaker's presentation.

1. _____ The summary was too long.

2. _____ The speaker used too many examples.

3. _____ The speaker presented her own ideas or opinions.

4. _____ The speaker did not use her own words, but lifted material from the reading.

Worksheet 4: Summary
Feedback Form for Class Member

Directions: Complete this form for one of the speakers in the class.

Name of Speaker _____

Topic _____

A. Rate the speaker on each point listed below by using the scale of 1 to 4.

Poor 1	2	3	Excellent 4

1. _____ The title and author were clearly stated at the beginning.

2. _____ The topic of the article was stated clearly and concisely.

3. _____ The examples chosen clearly supported their respective points.

4. _____ The speaker's pronunciation was clear and evenly paced.

B. Check the items below that apply to the speaker's presentation.

1. _____ The summary was too long.

2. _____ The speaker used too many examples.

3. _____ The speaker presented her own ideas or opinions.

4. _____ The speaker did not use her own words, but lifted material from the article.

Comments

Write any comments that you feel will help the speaker to give better verbal summaries in the future.

A woman who had been blind since birth underwent an eye operation that enabled her to see. As soon as she awoke from the operation, the doctor let her look at herself in a mirror. "Oh," she said, with some disappointment. "I thought I looked better than that."

How could she have had any idea of what she looked like? How could she even have known what "good-looking" meant? Apparently, even people who have been blind since birth have conceptions that resemble vision.

Kennedy (1983) asked some blind people to "draw pictures" with a kit designed so that they could make raised lines on a flat plastic sheet. None of them had ever tried to draw before. Still, without any instruction or practice, they drew outlines fairly similar to what a sighted person might draw. After feeling their drawings, they expressed surprise and satisfaction over their abilities. Figure 1 shows drawings that blind people made of a coat hanger, crossed fingers, and a water glass.

The perception of visual information by means of touch has been used in many vision-substitution systems for the blind. The braille system, for example, consists of patterns of raised dots (Figure 2), each pattern representing a number or a letter of the alphabet. Braille, which was devised in 1829, was not based on any research to discover the

Figure 1. Raised-line drawings made by blind people, representing a coat hanger, crossed fingers, and a water glass. (*From Kennedy, 1983.*)

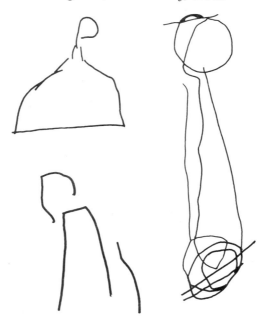

Figure 2. Braille symbols for the numbers 0–9.

```
. .      . .      . . .    . . .    . . .
.        . .      .        . . .    . . .
. .      . .      . .      . .      . .
 1        2        3        4        5
```

```
. . .    . . .    . .      . .      . . .
. . .    . . .    . . .    . .      . . .
. .      . .      . .      . .      . .
 6        7        8        9        0
```

kind of touch symbols that would be easiest to read. Although many blind people learn to read braille with some ease, it is a fairly difficult system to master.

Newman et al. (1982) conducted a series of experiments with sighted college students trying to learn braille. All were permitted to study the braille alphabet for as long as they wished. Some studied it by feeling the letters without looking at them. Others looked at a display of the Braille letters without feeling the dots. All were tested on their ability to recognize the raised dots by touch. Those who studied the patterns visually, without feeling the letters, spent only one-third as much time studying as those who studied by touching the letters. And yet they did better when tested on their ability to recognize the letters by touch! This is a very unusual example of learning one skill by practicing another. One implication is that the processing of braille and similar touch information uses intellectual processes similar to those involved in vision.

THE CONTRIBUTION OF TELEVISION TO CHILDREN'S DEVELOPMENT AND EDUCATION: COMMENTARY

Television. The word once called forth wondrous visions and terrible fears of what the medium would mean for American children. Optimists saw it as a master teacher, a window on the world, an activity uniting the family. Pessimists saw it as a time waster, a purveyor of distasteful content, an activity isolating each child with an electronic baby-sitter. Optimists sought to hasten television's arrival into the home; pessimists sought first to delay it and then to minimize its impact. It did not take long for the pessimists to fail, as during the 1960s television became a part of virtually every American household.

Now that a generation of television-reared children have become men and women rearing their own children with television, should the optimists of the past be glad? Did they accurately foresee the future? Some people today answer yes, and again yes. They point to television's contributions to children's development and education. Television brings physical processes and events, great people, faraway places and peoples, and important stories to life and makes them available to all children, even those who cannot read. It is as close to a real-life experience as children can get without being there. Sometimes it is actually better, because it can slow life down, repeat it, zoom in close to it, and move back from it. Television can even lead children to experience fear, anger, and disgust without ever having to suffer through the real-life experiences that would normally provoke such feelings. Finally, those who look on the bright side applaud the fact that most television viewing goes on in children's own homes, often with others in the room or close by, and that its content is a frequent topic of children's conversations with family and friends.

Hearing all these claims for the good that television does, the pessimists of yesterday and today clamor for an opportunity to present their side. They agree that televised presentations are lifelike, that even very young children can understand at least some of what is presented. At a minimum they can imitate the actions of characters on television. But "what characters and what actions!" the pessimists exclaim. They find much of what television presents and most of what children choose to view to be trivia and sometimes even trash. It is sex, violence, consumerism, ridicule, racism, sexism, and ageism—not the good things in life—that entertain children for several hours each day. Those who look on the dark side note that such entertainment is chosen in place of playing with other children, amusing oneself, studying, and doing chores.

Amid these conflicting claims about television, one easily asks where reality is. Clear-thinking men and women have argued this very point for decades now. You should too. Television programming is undeniably attractive to children, with information, stories, and advertisements that are easier to understand than are those in any other medium except film. Because television is a superb medium for presenting some aspects of the world to children, we should all be especially concerned about the programming menu it offers and the diet children choose. How can we make television content the best possible? How can we lead children to prefer the best? How can we teach them to interpret television's messages properly and use them wisely? And how can we be sure they spend enough time actively experiencing the world, mucking in it, and trying things out, not just sitting home watching the world go by on a large-size, full-color television screen?

Why worry about all this? At first thought a slightly warmer climate might seem desirable, resulting in longer growing seasons and possible increases in crop productivity in some parts of the world. The milder winters would also save fuel, although some of these savings would be canceled by increased use of air conditioning during the hotter summers.

Unfortunately along with benefits for some parts of the world there could be serious consequences in other areas. The projected change in average global temperature could modify the distribution of rainfall and snowfall over much of the earth, reduce the length of crop growing seasons in some parts of the world, and cause some melting of glaciers and ice fields in polar regions, which could cause sea levels to rise.

According to the 1983 NAS study, the most likely threat from global warming over the next 50 to 100 years would be shifts in food-growing regions and capacity during a time when the world's population is expected to at least double. Rainfall and snowfall patterns would shift, and some presently productive cropland would have to be abandoned and replaced with land of unknown quality. Existing irrigation and drainage systems and food storage and transportation systems that cost many billions of dollars would have to be rebuilt to reflect new patterns of precipitation. For example, Canada, the Soviet Union, the northeastern part of the United States, and some arid regions like the Sahel area in Africa might get more rain and thus eventually be able to grow more food than they do today. But for several decades there probably would be instability in global food production and distribution because many of the new crop-growing areas would have poor soils and would not be organized to farm, irrigate, store, and distribute large amounts of grain.

The U.S. wheat and corn belt in the Midwest and the irrigated farming areas of California and the Texas Gulf Coast would become much drier. Thus, much of the crop-growing regions in these parts of the United States might be replaced by such northern areas as the Saskatchewan Province in Canada, where the soils are poorer and less productive.

According to the 1983 NAS report, the even greater projected increase in temperature at the earth's poles would cause thermal expansion of warmer ocean water and some melting of the land-based Antarctic ice; hence average sea levels would rise about 0.70 meter (2.3 feet) over the next 100 years.

Eventually most, if not all, of the floating Arctic ice pack would probably melt, thus opening the northwest and northeast passages to ships through most of the year. Since this ice pack is afloat, its melting would not raise the water level in oceans—just as melting a floating ice cube in a glass does not raise the water level. But the absence of polar ice would change ocean currents and trigger unpredictable changes in the climate of the Northern Hemisphere.

Some of the land-based Antarctic glacial ice might melt slowly and cause a rise in average sea levels. Despite stories in the popular press predicting that the world's major coastal cities and floodplains (which produce most of the world's food) will soon be flooded, this melting process, if it occurred, would probably take place over several hundred years. A 1983 EPA report projected a maximum increase in average sea level of 3 meters (10 feet) and a most-probable rise of 2.4 meters (8 feet) by 2100.

SOME CONTROVERSIAL FOOD ADDITIVES

Three types of allegedly harmful additives are *food color dyes made from coal tar dyes, nitrates and nitrites,* and *sulfites.* Although natural pigments and dyes exist, most artificial food colors are obtained from coal tar dyes. In 1900 about 100 artificial dyes were in use in the United States, but evidence began accumulating that many of them cause cancer in test animals. By 1983 only six coal tar dyes were still approved by the FDA, and critics charge that these had not been tested adequately for safety. Even with this small number, public exposure to coal tar food dyes can be extensive. The FDA estimates that by age 12, 10 percent of all U.S. children have eaten over 454 grams (1 pound) of these dyes. About half the food additives that have been banned by the FDA have been coal tar dye food colorings.

Another controversial group of additives are nitrates and nitrites (mostly as sodium nitrate and sodium nitrite), added to most processed meats to retard spoilage, prevent botulism, enhance flavor, and improve color. Studies have shown that they may form N-nitroso compounds (nitrosoamines), which have been shown to cause cancer of the stomach and esophagus in animals. In 1978 the FDA and the Department of Agriculture created a stir when they proposed the gradual phasing out of these preservatives. Food industry officials and scientists, however, point out that this may not help because humans are exposed to even larger concentrations of nitrosoamines from other sources. For example, a pack of 20 filter cigarettes provides a nitrosoamine intake of about 17 micrograms and a single cigar 11 micrograms, compared to an average dietary intake of about 1.1 micrograms per day.

Nitrates and nitrites continued to be used in 1984 because of opposition to the ban from the food processing industry and because no substitutes had been found that are as effective as nitrates in preventing spoilage of some foods. While the search for such substitutes goes on, some scientists urge Americans to limit their consumption of bologna, salami, corned beef, hot dogs, bacon, and other cured and smoked meats. Even if nitrates and nitrites turn out to be harmless, these meats are high in sodium, which contributes to cardiovascular disease.

Sulfites are a group of widely used food preservatives that have been linked to acute allergic reactions in some people, especially about 5 percent of those with asthma (amounting to about 450,000 Americans). Sulfites are added to, or applied as a spray or dip to fresh fruits, vegetables, and shellfish by food wholesalers, grocery stores, and restaurants to retard spoilage and to keep the items looking fresh. Sulfites are also used in making beer and wine. People allergic to sulfites develop symptoms that include weakness, severe wheezing, labored breathing, coughing, extreme shortness of breath, blue discoloration of the skin, and loss of consciousness. In 1983 the FDA was planning to declare most sulfites safe. But after protests by consumer and physician groups the FDA recommended that state officials who have the responsibility for regulating food wholesalers, groceries, and restaurants insist that these businesses either cease using the additives or alert consumers to their use of sulfites by signs on grocery bins or notes on menus.

NEED FOR ACHIEVEMENT, FEAR OF FAILURE, AND GOAL-SETTING

We can contrast need for achievement with **fear of failure**. People whose fear of failure is much stronger than their need for achievement behave differently from people whose need for achievement is stronger than their fear of failure.

For example, people with a strong need for achievement usually set goals for themselves that are high but not unrealistic (Atkinson & Birch, 1978). In one study, students were asked to throw ten rings to try to hit a peg from any distance they chose, from 1 to 15 feet (0.3 to 4.6 meters). Since each student threw the rings as the others stood around watching, there was an element of competition even though no one was keeping score. Students who had scored high on need for achievement generally chose intermediate distances and managed to hit the peg a little less than half the time. So they were able to feel proud of each success. Students dominated by fear of failure, however, chose either very short distances, from which it was almost impossible to fail, or very long distances, which provided them with an excellent excuse for failing. Apparently, those with a strong fear of failure would rather fail at an impossible task than run the risk of failing at a realistic task.

People with a strong fear of failure will make a normal effort, or even an above-normal effort, on an easy task or in a relaxed, low-pressure situation. But if told, "This is an important test; you are going to be evaluated, so do your best," they make less effort. By contrast, people with a high need for achievement try harder (Nygard, 1982). ("Fear of failure" is often regarded as synonymous with "test anxiety.")

When people receive feedback on their performance, such as, "You got 82 percent correct on the first test," those with a high need for achievement usually increase their efforts, whereas those with a lower need do not increase their efforts and sometimes decrease them. Apparently, those with a high need for achievement set such high goals that they interpret almost any feedback as meaning that they are behind schedule and need to try harder (Matsui, Okada, & Kakuyama, 1982).

COGNITIVE DISSONANCE

You will sometimes hear people say, "If you want to change people's behavior, you have to change their attitudes first." Psychological research supports just the opposite conclusion: One of the most effective ways to change people's attitudes is to change their behavior first.

The theory behind this approach is known as **cognitive dissonance.** Dissonance means disharmony, conflict. Cognitive dissonance is a conflict between opposing thoughts. According to the theory of cognitive dissonance (Festinger, 1957), people try to minimize that conflict. A person who has contradictory attitudes, or who believes one thing and does another, experiences an unpleasant tension. He or she will try to reduce that tension by changing some of the attitudes or actions to bring them into harmony with the others.

People reduce the tension in several ways (Wicklund & Brehm, 1976). If you find that one of your actions is inconsistent with one of your attitudes, you may change your action, change your attitude, or add a new attitude that justifies your action under the circumstances. Generally, people change whatever they find easiest to change.

In an experiment to demonstrate cognitive dissonance, Festinger and Carlsmith (1959) invited 71 male undergraduates to take part in an experiment on "motor behavior." First each student was to place spools on a tray with one hand, then remove them, then put them back again, and so on for half an hour. Then he was given a board with 48 wooden pegs. For the next half-hour he was to take each peg, rotate it one quarter turn, and return it to the board. He was to repeat this process for all 48 pegs as many times as possible in the alloted time. Throughout the hour the experimenter watched the subject's behavior, took notes, and pretended to be interested in the speed and accuracy of performance. Actually, the tasks were chosen only because they were so boring.

At the end of the hour the experimenter thanked each subject and explained that one purpose of the study was to see whether performance was affected by the attitudes students brought to the experiment. Sitting outside in the waiting room was a young woman who, the experimenter explained, was to be the next subject. Ordinarily, the experimenter went on, an employee posing as an experimental subject went out and told the next subject that this was an interesting experiment, but unfortunately that employee could not come in today. "So," the experimenter asked, "Would you be willing to tell her that this was an interesting, enjoyable experiment? If so," he continued, "I will pay you."

Some students were offered one dollar; others were offered 20 dollars. Most agreed. (Three refused, saying they would not tell such a horrible lie for any price. Two agreed, then told the woman, "Hey, they paid me to say this was a fun experiment, but really I was bored to tears." Another told her it was interesting but insisted on getting her phone number so he could call her and "explain" later.)

Students who told the woman how much fun they had in this "delightful" experiment were asked by a representative of the psychology department to answer a few questions. The representative explained that the department wanted to find out what kinds of experiments were being conducted and whether they were educationally worthwhile. The answers to these questions were the real point of the experiment. Each student was asked, among other things, how enjoyable he considered the experiment and whether he would be willing to participate in a similar experiment later in the semester.

Which students do you think said they liked the experiment more, those who were paid 20 dollars or those who got only one dollar? The students who received 20 dollars said that frankly they thought the experiment was boring and that they wanted nothing to do with another such experiment. Those who received just a dollar said the experiment was really enjoyable and they would be glad to participate again.

Why? According to the theory of cognitive dissonance, those who accepted 20 dollars to tell someone the experiment was interesting experienced no conflict. They knew they were telling a lie, but they also knew why: They did it for the 20 dollars. (When this experiment took place, during the 1950s, 20 dollars was worth a lot more than it is today.) When they were asked for their real opinion of the experiment, they were quite ready to describe it as boring.

The students who told a lie for only a dollar, however, did experience cognitive dissonance. They knew there was a conflict between what they had felt (boredom) and what they had said ("It was a fun experiment"). They asked themselves, "Why did I say it was an enjoyable experiment? Was it for a measly dollar? Everyone has a price, I suppose, but I'd hate to think that mine is only one dollar!" Since it was too late to take back what they had said about the experiment, the only way they could minimize their cognitive dissonance was to change their attitude, to decide that the experiment really *was* somewhat interesting after all.

In a second experiment (Aronson & Carlsmith, 1963), four-year-old children (one child at a time) were shown five toys: a tank, a steam shovel, plastic gears, a fire engine, and a set of dishes and pans. Each child was asked which toy he or she thought was the best one, the second best, and so on. Then the experimenter said he would have to leave the room. He invited the child to play with the toys while he was gone, except, he insisted, "I don't want you to play with the _____," filling in whichever toy the child had ranked second. To some of the children, he made a mild threat: "If you played with it, I would be annoyed." To others he made a more severe threat: "If you played with it, I would be very angry. I would have to take all of my toys and go home and never come back again. . . . I would think you were just a baby. . . ."

The experimenter left for ten minutes and watched the child through a one-way mirror. None of the children played with the forbidden toy. Then he returned and asked the child to tell him again which was the best toy, the second best, and so on.

All the children who had received the severe threat ranked the forbidden toy either first or second. Almost half of the children who had received the mild threat lowered their evaluation of the forbidden toy. Why? Again the reason is cognitive dissonance. Those who avoided playing with their second-favorite toy because of the severe threat knew perfectly well why they were not playing with it. Those who avoided it because of the mild threat were not so sure. "Am I staying away from that toy just because that man said he would be annoyed if I played with it?" Because that did not sound like much of a reason, many of the children convinced themselves that they did not really like the toy very much anyhow.

RISE IN COHABITATION

As you may have guessed, a rising age at marriage has not meant that people are avoiding sexual unions altogether. Au contraire. The rise in cohabitation (living together) has indeed been one of the most prominent recent changes that has led to a belief that the family is dying. It is pretty easy to see why the demise seems imminent to some, since the number of unmarried couples in the United States more than tripled from half a million in 1970 to nearly 2 million in 1982. The most dramatic increase, not surprisingly, has been among younger adults. The Baby Boom cohort increased the number of unmarried couples under age 45 twelvefold between 1970 and 1982. In 1970 there were only 89,000 unmarried couples under age 45, and they accounted for only 17 percent of all unmarried couples; by 1982, there were 1,087,000 unmarried couples under 45, and they represented 58 percent of all unmarried couples. During that time there was little change in the incidence of living together among people aged 45 and older (U.S. Bureau of the Census, 1983b).

The increase in cohabitation is not due simply to the increase in the number of young adults. Note that in 1970 there were 72 million Americans aged 18–44 and the number increased to 98 million in 1982—a 36 percent increase. However, there was a 1,121 percent increase in the number of unmarried couples aged 18–44. Remember, though, that unmarried couples represent only a small fraction of all couples; in fact, in 1982 the 1,087,000 unmarried couples under age 45 represented only about 4 percent of all couples under 45. Yet the proportion is rising rapidly, and it is likely that these figures on current cohabitation "considerably understate the percentage of young persons who will cohabit at some time during their lives. Eighteen percent of a 1974–75 sample of men in their twenties said they had lived with a woman without marriage for six months or more, even though only 5 percent were currently cohabiting" (Thornton & Freedman, 1983:12).

Since women now have the potential for greater independence, they may also be less willing to commit themselves to a relationship until they have tried it out for a while. For both sexes, cohabitation can be a way of avoiding the emotional and financial responsibility that might be involved in a marriage. The avoidance of family responsibility is, of course, facilitated by the now widespread use of effective contraceptives and abortion, and in the United States and most of western Europe levels of fertility tend to be lower among cohabiting couples than among the married (Klimas Blanc, 1984). In Sweden and Denmark, however, where as many as 20 percent of all couples may be cohabiting (Westoff, 1978b), childbearing within such unions is much more common.

EARLY GENDER–ROLE INFLUENCES

Gender roles (or sex roles) are defined by the particular combination of attitudes, behaviors, and personality characteristics that a culture considers appropriate for the individual's anatomical sex—in other words, what is considered *masculine* or *feminine.* Sex-typing, or gender typing, is the psychological expression used to describe the process whereby boys and girls learn masculine and feminine roles.

Although it might be tempting to think that masculinity and femininity are primarily the products of genetically ordained physiological and hormonal differences between males and females, there is considerable evidence that this is only partly the case. In some cultures—for example, the Tchambuli described by Margaret Mead (1935)—behaviors that we might consider feminine are expected of men and are therefore masculine; at the same time, the aggressiveness and dominance that we think of as masculine characterize women (see Chapter 12 for more details). Clearly, cultures and families have a great deal to do with the eventual gender roles of their children.

When does sex-typing begin? At the very beginning. When an infant is born, the attending physician or midwife doesn't say, "Holy Jeepers, lady, it's a *baby!*"

No. The key word is not *baby*—it's "boy" or "girl." The simple anatomical fact of being boy or girl tells mother and father and all the significant others what to think and how to react. The knowledge that it's a "boy" or "girl" even colors the parents' perceptions. When Rubin, Provenzano, and Luria (1974) asked 30 parents to describe their day-old infants as they would to a relative or a close friend, without any hesitation they spoke of their alert, strong, well-coordinated, firm, and hardy sons. In contrast, they described their daughters as weaker, finer-featured, softer, less attentive, more delicate. Yet these parents, especially the fathers (who were most guilty of exaggerating the sex-appropriate characteristics of their sons), had scarcely had any opportunity to interact with and get to know their infants. And hospital records indicated clearly that these male and female infants were *indistinguishable* one from the other in terms of weight, muscle tone, activity, responsiveness, and so on.

Pogrebin (1980), in a provocative consideration of these issues, suggests that we are a little like the Mundugumor of New Guinea—one of three tribes studied by Margaret Mead in her investigation of sex and temperament. The Mundugumor believed that a variety of signs could be used at birth to predict what the individual would become. For example, they were convinced that only those infants whose umbilical cords were wound around their necks at birth stood any chance of becoming great artists. Amazingly, they were right! All Mundugumor artists whose talents were accepted as outstanding had, in fact, been born with their umbilical cords twisted around their necks.

Our fortune-telling is not so primitive, is it? We know it's ridiculous to think that the position of the umbilical cord is of any consequence. Instead, we look for appendages between the legs of our infants. To a considerable extent, these tell us how to interact with our infants, what to expect of them, what sorts of toys they are most likely to enjoy, what their personalities should be. Their presence or absence also allows us to predict whether the infant will grow up to be strong and alert and aggressive—or weaker, more delicate, more sensitive, more emotional. And amazingly often, our predictions are every bit as accurate as those of the Mundugumor.

Research suggests there may be some reason to question the ancient assumption that all children are highly fragile and that the development of their personalities and their eventual adjustment are entirely in the hands of their parents. But it would be more than a little foolish to assert that parents do not make any difference. Clearly, they do.

Several other variables, some of them far more easily measured than parenting styles and parent–child relationships, might also be important to the eventual outcome of the developmental process.

Among these is **birth order**, the position a child occupies in the family. Galton (1896) was among the first to note the effects of birth order when he observed that there was a preponderance of firstborn children among great British scientists. Since then, research has attributed many advantages to being the firstborn (or an only child). Among them are more rapid and more articulate language development, higher scores on measures of intellectual performance, higher scores on measures of achievement motivation, better academic performance, more curiosity, and a higher probability of going to college (see Melican & Feldt, 1980; Page & Grandon, 1979; Ernst & Angst, 1983). And, for what it's worth, the probability of a firstborn child going into space seems considerably higher than that of a later-born child (*Newsweek*, 1969).

There are a number of plausible explanations for the observed effects of birth order. Certainly, these effects are not due simply to being a firstborn, a middle, or a lastborn child, but to the fact that the interactions and relationships to which the child is exposed are, at least to some extent, determined by position in the family. As Zajonc and Markus (1975) point out, a firstborn child enjoys a close relationship with two adult models. It is hardly surprising that language development should be more accelerated under these conditions than it might be if the child had been born later or had been one member of a multiple birth. In these latter cases, the parents have less time to interact with the child, and other nonadult models are now an important part of the family environment.

Before we go running off bragging that we're firstborns or only children—or complaining that we're not—we should note that the contribution of birth order to intelligence and academic achievement may, after all, be quite negligible. Following a massive investigation of 9,000 high school students and their brothers and sisters (a total of more than 30,000 subjects), Hauser and Sewell (1985) found that the importance of birth order was quite trivial. What appears to be important is not whether you are firstborn or later-born, but the size of your family.

FOLK AND ETHNIC MUSIC

The words *folk* and *ethnic* are not synonymous. **Ethnic** refers to music identified with a particular group of people. **Folk music** refers only to music actually created or adopted by the common people. A Hungarian peasant song about harvesting hay is a folk song, and, because it is characteristic of that country, it is also ethnic music. The *raga* of India is not folk music; it is not the music of the common people but rather of a highly trained musical elite. It is characteristic of India, though, so it is ethnic music. Therefore, all folk music is ethnic, but not all ethnic music is folk music.

Generally speaking, folk–ethnic music is functional music. It is usually valued not for its musical qualities but rather according to how well it fulfills its task of persuading spirits, accompanying the telling of a story, or providing a sense of group solidarity. The music may have considerable beauty in itself, but artistic expression is not the chief goal for most folk–ethnic music.

Creation

Contrary to popular belief, there is little "community composition"— music created by a group of people sitting around a campfire or marching into battle. Individuals create ethnic music, just as individuals compose art music. But there the similarity ends. The creators of ethnic music are almost always unknown. In fact, the individual might not admit to the accomplishment even if he or she could be located. In many areas of the world songs are supposed to be gifts from the gods revealed in dreams or visions or created on orders from a supernatural being. Besides, in most cultures people neither care nor remember who was first responsible for a song.

Oral Tradition

Once created, the music is perpetuated through **oral tradition**, whereby individuals hear the music, remember it, and perform it for others. If no one except the originator likes the song, it passes into oblivion. This tradition ensures the survival of only those songs that are liked by the particular culture. Oral tradition also means that the music is subject to many changes. Suppose that three people hear a song and that one of them is very musical. That person remembers it clearly, but decides to make a few small improvements in it. The second person also remembers the song clearly. But he or she belongs to another culture and adapts the song for use in that culture by setting new words to it and altering its rhythm and melody. The third person is not so musical, forgets half of the song, and sings the remembered portion inaccurately. The result is that what started out as one song is now three songs. And each of these versions will in turn be subjected to a similar process of revision and alteration.

Nonliterate societies have no system of musical notation. Even in the advanced societies of ancient India and China, only a system of visual cues was developed. Without a system of notation or recordings, music cannot be preserved exactly. For this reason, folk music is ever changing, which may be one of its strengths. It represents the heritage of the people and also their current tastes.

Relationship with Culture

A thorough study of ethnic and folk music is a complicated undertaking. The music is only the beginning. The total culture must be included—language, customs, thought forms, and so on. Ethnic music cannot be separated from the culture in which it exists. For example, among the Yoruba tribe in Africa, each type of drum represents one or more deities, and each deity has its own distinctive rhythm. The rituals can be understood only by a person who knows the particular drums, rhythms, and appropriate god. Some Indian scholars object to attempts to illustrate ragas in musical notation and to discuss their musical aspects. To do so, they maintain, is to leave out the vital spiritual aspects of the music.

Complexity

Most of the folk–ethnic music of the world is less complex than art music. Why? First, most of it consists of short works, usually songs. True, some African rituals last for hours, but the same music tends to be repeated over and over, with only slight variations. The Indian raga is also long, but it is an exceptional kind of music. Without a system of notation, musical works are usually rather short-winded. The short length allows for little development of themes, something that is important to art music.

When ethnic music does display complexity, such as in the rhythm of African music, it tends to do so with only one aspect of the music, leaving the other aspects relatively undeveloped. By contrast, art music often consists of complicated combinations of pitch, harmony, rhythm, timbre, dynamics, and form.

The roots of **jazz** reach back to black Americans' African heritage. But other elements have also influenced jazz: minstrel show music, work songs, field hollers, funeral marching bands, blues, French-Creole and Spanish-American music, and more recently, West Indian music. Jazz did not develop until about the beginning of the twentieth century. Basin Street in New Orleans is traditionally considered its birthplace, although clearly jazz did not just pop into being in one spot and at a fixed historical moment. It was brought to public attention by the funeral procession. On the way back from the cemetery the band played tunes in a way quite different from the somber sounds that accompanied the march to the gravesite. The players shifted the emphasis from the strong to the weak beat and launched into a decorated version of the melody. When Storyville, the New Orleans red-light district, was closed down in 1917, many jazz musicians lost their jobs and sought work in other cities. Jazz moved up the Mississippi River through Memphis and St. Louis to Chicago and the rest of the United States.

Two types of Afro-American folk music existed before and during the early years of jazz and later merged with it. One of these was **ragtime**. It featured the piano, occasionally in combination with other instruments. The music sounds like a polished, syncopated march with a decorated right-hand part. Early musicians associated with ragtime are Scott Joplin in Sedalia, Missouri, and Ben Harvey, who published his *Ragtime Instructor* in 1897.

The other type of music involved with early jazz was the folk **blues**. Its musical characteristics will be discussed shortly. Some of the most famous names associated with blues are Leadbelly, whose real name was Huddie Ledbetter; W. C. Handy, who was known for his "Memphis Blues" and "St. Louis Blues"; and Ferdinand "Jelly Roll" Morton, whose first published blues appeared in 1905—the "Jelly Roll Blues."

Like folk music, jazz was created by generally untutored musicians who could not have written down what they played or sang, even if they had wanted to. Jazz is different from most folk music in two respects, however. It has sprung from the cities rather than the fields and forests; it is an urban form of music. And for most people, it is a spectator experience. Usually only a few people perform, although listeners may contribute a little hand clapping and foot stomping.

7

Giving a
Formal Talk

—— What Will You Do in This Chapter? ——

In this chapter you will learn to give a formal talk on basic concepts from your academic field or profession.

—— Why Is It Important to Practice Giving a Formal Talk? ——

It is important that you be comfortable with speaking in a formal context because you will often be called on to speak as an expert in your profession as well as in academia.

—— How Should You Organize Your Talk? ——

You should state your topic as a question and organize the body of the talk as an answer to this question. The strategy of posing your topic as a question not only focuses the audience immediately on the topic but also makes it easier for them to follow the talk.

Following are examples of topic questions:

Today I'd like to talk to you about an interesting topic in linguistics. What is language?

My topic is the origins of alcoholism. What causes this addiction?

Having presented your topic as a question, you will organize the body of your talk as an answer to this question. There are three effective ways to organize the information in the body of a formal talk:

1. by using clear, concrete examples that illustrate the topic,

2. by discussing the important characteristics of the topic, or

3. by comparing or contrasting the topic with another concept.

When constructing an answer to your topic question, choose the technique(s) for structuring information that make it possible for you to give an accurate and complete discussion of your topic. If your topic is complex, you might find it helpful to use two or even all three of these techniques.

Following are examples of two talks. The first illustrates a talk supported by listing major characteristics. The second uses examples and comparisons.

—— Example 1: A Formal Talk Organized by Listing Major Characteristics ——

Topic

Today I'd like to talk to you about an interesting topic in linguistics. What is language?

Answer

While this is a rather broad topic, today I'd like to limit my comments to only two major characteristics that define language. (**major characteristic:**) The first characteristic of language is that it is a system. . . . [explanation]. . . . (**major characteristic:**) The second characteristic of language that I would like to talk about today is that there is an arbitrary relationship between sound and meaning in any language. . . . [explanation]. . . .

——Example 2: A Formal Talk
Organized by Using Concrete
Examples and Comparisons ——

Topic

My topic is the origins of alcoholism. What causes this addiction?

Answer

I'd like to focus on two major explanations for the cause of alcoholism. The first position claims that alcoholism has a genetic origin. (**example:**) For example, a study conducted at _____ Hospital found that all the alcoholics in treatment had at least one parent who also suffered from the condition. (**comparison:**) This is very similar to the research done at _____ Medical School, which found that obese patients came from families with at least one obese parent. The second position on the roots of alcoholism states that this is a social disease. (**example:**) Statistics cited by _____ and _____ show that. . . . (**comparison:**) Again, similarities were found with other addictions. . . . Evidence shows that drug addicts learn the behaviors associated with their disease just as smokers learn the behaviors associated with their addiction. . . .

Note: Often a formal presentation like the ones described in this chapter is followed by a question and answer session in which audience members have the chance to interact with the speaker. Strategies for participating in a question and answer session are discussed in Chapter 8.

——Sample Expressions Used
When Presenting a Concept ——

■ Introductory Remarks

Today I'd like to talk to you about an interesting topic in the field of

_____ . What is (a) _____ ?

I'm going to talk to you today about one of the fundamental issues in

(the field of) _____ .

What is the definition of _____ ?

■ Giving Examples

To show what I mean, let's look at an example.

(continued)

In order to illustrate this concept, I'd like to look at _____ .

An example of what I am talking about is _____ .

For example, _____ .

■ Listing Major Characteristics

While this is a rather broad topic, I would like to limit my comments to only two major characteristics/approaches/topics.

The first characteristic of _____ is _____ .

The second characteristic of _____ is _____ .

■ Comparing or Contrasting Concepts

In order to better understand _____ , we can compare it to

another concept, _____ .

This is similar to _____ . They both _____ .

This is different from what we found when we studied _____ .

——— Assignments ———

Assignment 1: Preparation of a Formal Talk

In this assignment you will prepare a five to seven minute formal talk on a topic in your academic field or profession and practice it with a classmate.

1. Choose a topic from the list below. These topics are only suggestions; you may choose another topic with the approval of your instructor.

2. Use Worksheet 1 to prepare your talk. Formulate your topic as a question and organize the body of your talk as an answer to your question. Use the sample expressions on pp. 113–114. Your teacher will give you feedback on the topic you have selected and on the approach(es) you have chosen to present your information.

3. Practice your presentation on your own. If possible, use a tape recorder.

4. After you have practiced your presentation at least twice on your own, give your presentation to a classmate who will give you feedback on the clarity of your talk using Worksheet 2.

Topics for Assignment 1

Anthropology: What is culture?
                  What is the relationship between language and
                      world view?

Art   What is originality in art?
                  What is postmodernism?

Business: How is profit best maximized?
                  What is a recession?
                  What is supply and demand?
                  What constitutes a management style in business?

Chemistry: What is titration?
                  What is a gas?

Psychology: What is schema?
                  What is perception?

Computer Science: What is a computer language?
                  What is an algorithm?

Engineering: What is motion?
                  What is equilibrium?

Linguistics: What is language?
                  What is grammar?

Literature: What is literary criticism?
                  What is poststructuralism?

Math: What is a set?
                  What is a function?

Philosophy: What is ontology?
                  What is reason?

Physics: What is energy?
                  What is a vector?
                  What does the conservation of energy really
                      mean?

Political Science: What constitutes a political system?
                   What is a political party?
                   What is chemical warfare?

Psychology: What is short-term memory?
                  What is behaviorism?
                  What does the term alcoholism really mean?

Religious Studies: What is a cult?
                   What are some universal religious concepts?

Sociology: What is a society?
                  What are the elements of a social class?

Statistics: What is probability?
                  What is statistical significance?

Assignment 2: Presentation of a Formal Talk to the Class

In this assignment, you will present your talk to the entire class.

1. Present your talk to the class. You may use your notes from Worksheet 1.

2. Your teacher will designate two of your classmates (other than your partner) to give you feedback on your talk using Worksheet 3.

Worksheet 1:
Preparation of a Formal Talk

Directions: Use this worksheet to prepare your presentation.

1. **Topic:**
   Formulate your topic as a question.

   _____

   _____

   _____

2. **Body of the talk:**
   Identify the way you will organize the information in your talk by placing a check next to the technique(s) you will use.

examples	
characteristics	
comparison/contrast	
other	

   Use the space below to organize the body of your talk.

Worksheet 2: Formal Talk: Feedback Form for Partner

Directions: Complete this form after listening to your partner's formal talk.

Name of speaker: _____

Topic: _____

1. Was the topic question clear?

2. Identify the way(s) the speaker organized the information in the body of her talk by placing a check next to the technique(s) used.

examples	
characteristics	
comparison/contrast	
other	

3. Was there enough information provided in the body of the talk to explain the topic adequately? Comment on this.

4. Were you able to follow the discussion easily? If not, what suggestions can you make to help the speaker improve the clarity of her talk? (pronunciation, content, body language, speed of delivery)

Worksheet 3: Formal Talk: Feedback Form for Class Member

Directions: Your teacher will ask you to complete this form after listening to one of your classmates give her formal talk.

Name of speaker: _____

Topic: _____

1. Was the topic question clear?

2. Identify the way(s) the speaker organized the information in the body of her talk by placing a check next to the technique(s) used.

examples	
characteristics	
comparison/contrast	
other	

3. Was there enough information provided in the body of the talk to explain the topic adequately? Comment on this.

4. Were you able to follow the discussion easily? If not, what suggestions can you make to help the speaker improve the clarity of her talk? (pronunciation, content, body language, speed of delivery)

8

Asking and Answering Questions Following a Formal Talk

What Will You Do in This Chapter?

A formal talk is almost always followed by a question and answer session during which time the speaker responds to audience members' questions and comments. In this chapter, you will learn strategies for participating in the question and answer session that follows a formal talk. You will learn how to ask questions appropriately as an audience member and to respond appropriately as the presenter.

Why Are These Skills Important?

The way the interaction proceeds in the question and answer session often determines not only how the presenter is evaluated as a professional but also how audience members are perceived among their peers. It is therefore of great value to know how to participate skillfully in both these roles.

How Is the Transition Made from the Formal Talk to the Question and Answer Session?

The transition from the talk to the question and answer session is made when the presenter (1) signals that her talk has ended and (2) announces that she is available to respond to audience members' questions.

Following are some examples of transitions.

Example 1

Transitional phrase:	I think I'll close here.
Invitation for questions:	Does anyone have any questions?

Example 2

Transitional phrase:	That concludes my talk for today.
Invitation for questions:	Are there any questions?

Example 3

Transitional phrase:	This is a good time to end my part of the presentation.
Invitation for questions:	I'd like to open up the floor for questions and discussion.

Example 4

Transitional phrase:	I'd like to stop here
Invitation for questions:	and take questions.

What Are the *Questions* That Follow a Formal Talk Like?

Questions that follow a formal talk are different from other types of questions because they have two parts: (1) **a structuring move** and (2) **a question move**.

1. **The structuring move:** In the structuring move, the speaker identifies the topic of her question.

2. **The question move:** In the question move, the speaker asks her question. The question can be either a direct question or an indirect question.

Following are examples of questions that follow a talk on the topic "What is language?" Note that Examples 1 and 2 use direct questions and example 3 uses an indirect question.

Example 1

Structuring move:	I have a question about your definition of system.
Question move:	Is the dance of bees the same kind of system that language is?

Example 2

Structuring move:	I didn't understand the second characteristic of language that you described.
Question move:	What exactly did you mean by arbitrary?

Example 3

Structuring move:	I thought your talk was clear and informative, but
Question move:	I still have a question about what a system is.

—— What Are the *Answers* to the Questions That Follow a Formal Talk Like? ——

Answers to questions that follow a formal talk also have two parts: (1) **a responding move** and (2) **an expanding move.**

1. **The responding move:** The responding move answers the question briefly.

2. **The expanding move:** The expanding move provides additional information. The amount of information provided in the expanding move will depend on the speaker's knowledge of the topic and the time allowed.

Following are responses to the questions in Examples 1, 2, and 3 above. Note that the responding moves in Examples 1 and 3 are brief while the responding move in Example 2 is longer.

Example 1

Question	I have a question about your definition of system. Is the dance of bees the same kind of system that language is?

Answer

Responding move: No, it is not the same kind of system as I see it.

Expanding move: The dance of bees is a type of communication, but it differs from a human language system in several ways. . . . Other interesting communication systems include those of dolphins and whales.

Example 2

Question   I didn't understand the second characteristic of language that you described. What exactly did you mean by arbitrary?

Answer

Responding move: This is an important distinction. Let me see if I can clarify it for you. Arbitrariness in language refers to the relationship between a sound and its meaning.

Expanding move: We say this relationship is arbitrary because. . . .

Example 3

Question   I thought your talk was clear and informative, but I still have a question about what a system is.

Answer

Responding move: When we talk about a system, we're talking about something that is rule-governed.

Expanding move: In linguistics, specifically, a system refers to how sounds and words are combined according to a set of rules that speakers use to communicate with each other in a meaningful way. For example, one of these rules is. . . .

 — Sample Expressions Used for Making the Transition from the Formal Talk to the Question and Answer Session ——

■ **Transitional Phrase**

I think I'll close here.

This is a good place to stop.

I'd like to conclude my remarks here.

(continued)

That concludes my talk.

And with this final comment I would like to conclude.

I see we have only ten minutes left.

I'd like to save some time for questions so I'll end my talk here.

■ **Invitation for Questions**

I would be glad to answer any questions you might have.

Are there any questions?

Does anybody have any questions?

I'm happy to take questions at this point.

I'd like to open it up for questions.

 —— **Sample Expressions Used When Structuring a Question** ————

I have a question about your definition of _____ .

I thought your talk was clear, but _____ .

In the beginning of your talk you said _____ .

I didn't understand part of your definition of _____ .

In my work I considered a similar problem with _____ .

In my business we have problems with _____ also.

I disagree with your position on _____ .

 —— **Sample Expressions Used When Asking Questions** ————

What exactly did you mean by _____ ?

Could you explain _____ ?

(continued)

What did you mean by _____ ?

I didn't understand what you meant by _____ .

I have a question about _____ .

How can you defend your position in light of the new research?

 ── **Sample Expressions That Can Be Used in the Responding Move** ─────────

That's a good question.

This is an important distinction.

Let me see if I can clarify it for you. I think _____ .

Perhaps an example will help clarify that. My research indicates _____

_____ .

This question has a complex answer. My understanding is _____

_____ .

That's not an easy question to answer. It seems that _____

_____ .

I can further explain this by saying _____ .

I can illustrate this by giving you several examples. The first example is

_____ .

Some additional background on this topic helps to clarify the point I'm trying

to make. For example _____ .

 Furthermore, _____ .

Assignment 1: Preparation of Questions That Follow a Formal Talk

In this activity you will formulate questions that follow a formal talk. To prepare for this activity you must imagine that you are an audience member who has just heard a formal talk and that you are interested in asking two questions in the question and answer session.

1. Select five topics from the list below. For each topic imagine that you have just listened to a speaker give a formal talk and that the speaker has just called for questions.

2. Using the structuring and question moves described on pp. 127–128 formulate two questions that you might ask during the question and answer period following each talk that you have just "heard." Remember that since you have not actually heard each talk, you must "create" the content of each talk so that you can ask questions that are appropriate. Do not write the talk, just imagine it. Use Worksheet 1.

3. Have your teacher go over your questions.

Topics for Assignment 1

Anthropology:	What is culture?
	What is the relationship between language and world view?
Art	What is originality in art?
	What is postmodernism?
Business:	How is profit best maximized?
	What is a recession?
	What is supply and demand?
	What constitutes a management style in business?
Chemistry:	What is titration?
	What is a gas?
Psychology:	What is schema?
	What is perception?
Computer Science:	What is a computer language?
	What is an algorithm?
Engineering:	What is motion?
	What is equilibrium?
Linguistics:	What is language?
	What is grammar?
Literature:	What is literary criticism?
	What is poststructuralism?
Math:	What is a set?
	What is a function?

Philosophy:	What is ontology?
	What is reason?
Physics:	What is energy?
	What is a vector?
	What does the conservation of energy really mean?
Political Science:	What constitutes a political system?
	What is a political party?
	What is chemical warfare?
Psychology:	What is short-term memory?
	What is behaviorism?
	What does the term alcoholism really mean?
Religious Studies:	What is a cult?
	What are some universal religious concepts?
Sociology:	What is a society?
	What are the elements of a social class?
Statistics:	What is probability?
	What is statistical significance?

Assignment 2: Roleplaying the Transition to the Question and Answer Session and Asking Questions

With a partner, you will now roleplay a portion of the question and answer period that follows a formal talk using the questions you have formulated in Assignment 1. It is important to remember that the person taking the role of the presenter will neither give a formal talk nor actually answer any questions. She will simply open up the question and answer session to give you, as the audience member, the chance to practice asking questions.

1. Follow the example below for this exercise. The person taking the role of the presenter will write transitional phrases to the question and answer session for each of the five topics her partner chose in Assignment 1 using the sample expressions on pp. 126–127.

2. Use this format until the person taking the role of the audience member has asked all of her questions, and then switch roles.

Example:

Presenter:

Transitional phrase:	That concludes my talk "What does alcoholism mean?"
Invitation for questions:	I'd be happy to answer any questions you might have.

Audience member:

Structuring move: In the beginning of your talk, you said that there are two kinds of alcoholics.

Question move: Could you explain what you meant by a genetic predisposition for alcoholism?

Assignment 3: Presentation of a Formal Talk Followed by a Question and Answer Session

In this assignment you will prepare a four minute formal talk on a topic in your academic field or profession and present it to a group. (Refer to Chapter 7 for techniques on preparing a formal talk.) At the end of your talk, members of the group will ask questions for you to answer.

1. Choose a topic from the list on pp. 129–130. These topics are only suggestions; you may choose another topic with the approval of your instructor.

2. Use Worksheet 2 to prepare your talk. Follow the format used in Chapter 7: formulate your topic as a question and the body of your talk as an answer to the question.

3. After practicing your talk, you will present it to your group. Each member of the group will ask you a question following your talk. Use the techniques for asking and answering questions discussed in this chapter.

Assignment 4: Class Discussion

Use Worksheet 3 to prepare for a discussion of issues related to participation in a formal presentation and question and answer session.

Worksheet 1: Preparation of Questions That Follow a Formal Talk

Directions: Use this worksheet to practice formulating questions that follow a formal talk.

Topic 1: _____

_____

Structuring move:

Question move:

Topic 2: _____

_____

Structuring move:

Question move:

Topic 3: _____

_____

Structuring move:

Question move:

Topic 4: _____

_____

Structuring move:

Question move:

Topic 5: _____

_____

Structuring move:

Question move:

Worksheet 2:
    Preparation of a Formal Talk —————————————

Directions: Use this worksheet to prepare your presentation and the transition to the question and answer session.

1. Topic:

   Formulate your topic as a question.

   _____

   _____

2. Body of the talk:

   Identify the way you will organize the information in your talk by placing a check next to the technique(s) you will use.

examples	
characteristics	
comparison/contrast	
other	

3. Outline and/or write out the body of your talk in the space below.

4. Write out a transition phrase to the question and answer session.

── **Worksheet 3:**
     Class Discussion ─────────────────

Directions: Write short answers to the following questions and be prepared to discuss them with the class.

1. As the presenter, were you able to tell that a question was asked, especially when it was an indirect question?

2. As the presenter, did you find it easy to elaborate on an answer in the expanding move?

3. As the audience member, was it easy for you to combine a structuring move with a question move? Did the structuring move help you focus your question?

4. As an audience member, did you recognize when a question was asked and answered and when it was appropriate for another question to be asked?

5. Have you noticed the use of structuring moves in any other context where questions were being asked? (telephone conversations, class discussions, informal conversations)

C H A P T E R
9

Giving an Unrehearsed Talk

What Will You Do in This Chapter?

This chapter moves from the highly structured activities of previous chapters to a less structured yet very important speaking activity, the unrehearsed talk. You will practice speaking on various topics first with minimal preparation and finally without any previous preparation.

What Is an Unrehearsed Talk?

An unrehearsed talk is a talk given without preparation. Since you will often be called on to speak without preparation in a variety of both formal and informal professional contexts, it is important for you to be able to put your thoughts together "on-the-spot."

What Should You Be Thinking about When You Give Your Unrehearsed Talks?

When giving your unrehearsed talks, your focus should simply be on expressing your thoughts and opinions as clearly, concisely, and naturally as you can. The goal is to gain skill and ease with this type of speaking, not to perfect a format or to demonstrate the breadth of your knowledge of a topic. Try to have a good time just speaking with your classmates.

Sample Expressions for the Unrehearsed Talk

My feeling about this is _____ .

It has been my experience that _____ .

I think _____ .

I don't know very much about this but _____ .

In my experience, _____ .

In my country, _____ .

For me, _____ .

I don't have any experience with this firsthand, but I have heard/read that

_____

_____ .

In my family, _____

_____ .

This is a very broad topic.

Assignments

Assignment 1: An Unrehearsed Talk

In this activity, you will work in a group of three. Each member of the group will give a short unrehearsed talk on the same topic.

1. Select a topic from the list below with your group members. Each of you should take one minute to jot down some notes on the topic you have selected. Use the sample expressions above. Put your notes away.

2. Talk for one minute on this topic. Remember that your goal is simply to express your ideas briefly and clearly "on-the-spot."

Topics for Assignment 1:

dating customs

attitudes toward energy use

opportunities for higher education

family finances
gambling
economic conditions
political climate
attitudes toward television
censorship of the media
religious attitudes
immigrant populations
care of the elderly
treatment of mental health conditions
attitudes toward women
attitudes toward children
use of advanced technology in business
nuclear arms buildup or disarmament
use of nuclear power

Assignment 2: An Unrehearsed Talk

In this activity, you will work in groups of five and give a talk without any time to prepare your comments.

1. Your teacher will determine the order of the speakers and will ask a different group member to provide the topic for each talk. The topics may be taken from Assignment 1 or may be original topics prepared by group members.

2. You will have two minutes to give your unrehearsed talk. This time you will not be given any time to make notes before you speak.

3. After each talk, group members may want to ask questions or make comments.

Assignment 3: Class Discussion

Complete Worksheet 1 in preparation for a class discussion on unrehearsed talks.

Worksheet 1: Class Discussion on Unrehearsed Talks

Directions: Write short answers to the following questions.

1. Did you find it easy to put your thoughts together "on-the-spot"? Why or why not?

2. Were you able to speak with precision on your topics? Or did you feel that you were not able to get your points across to the listeners? Explain.

3. What did you find most challenging about speaking without preparation? Discussing the particular topic? Speaking in a second language? Speaking in front of a group? Speaking without having the chance to formulate your ideas first? Explain.

4. Do you think that being able to speak "on-the-spot" is a valuable skill? Explain.